THE
PRESIDENTIAL
BOOK ⭐ OF LISTS

THE PRESIDENTIAL BOOK OF LISTS

*From Most to Least, Elected to Rejected,
Worst to Cursed—Fascinating Facts
About Our Chief Executives*

IAN RANDAL STROCK

VILLARD BOOKS · NEW YORK

A Villard Books Trade Paperback Original

Copyright © 2008 by Ian Randal Strock

Published in the United States by Villard Books, an imprint of The Random
House Publishing Group, a division of Random House, Inc., New York.

VILLARD and "V" CIRCLED Design are registered trademarks
of Random House, Inc.

Library of Congress Cataloging-in-Publication Data

Strock, Ian Randal.
The presidential book of lists: from most to least, elected to rejected, worst
to cursed—fascinating facts about our chief executives / Ian Randal Strock.
        p.   cm.
Includes index.
ISBN 978-0-345-50736-5 (pbk.)
1. Presidents—United States—Miscellanea.   I. Title.
E176.1.S925 2008
973.09'9—dc22   2008028087

Printed in the United States of America

www.villard.com

2   4   6   8   9   7   5   3

Book design by Susan Turner

I dedicate this book to my family—the Strocks, Wagners, Silvermans,
Schenkers/Shenkers, Kesslers, Hawkinses, and Huddlestons—
all of whom played a role in making me who I am,
and making this book what it is, and none of whom,
so far as we can tell, are related to anyone discussed in this book.

CONTENTS

HOME AND FAMILY

RÉSUMÉ

ON THE JOB

AWARDS AND HONORS

OTHER PRESIDENTIAL INFORMATION

INTRODUCTION

I AM FASCINATED BY THE PRESIDENTS OF THE UNITED STATES OF America—and the presidency, and pretty much everything about our government. Created in the late 1700s, it was designed incredibly well: able to weather the vagaries of external and internal wars, good and bad Presidents, and happy and sad times in the country. Through it all, our government has survived, and our Presidents have become legends. Even after reading biographies, studying history books, and visiting their libraries and museums, I wanted more, and I turned to fiction about the Presidents as well.

I've been enthralled by books such as *The Man*, *The President's Plane is Missing*, and Tom Clancy's Jack Ryan series; movies such as *The American President*, *My Fellow Americans*, and *Air Force One*; and television series such as *The West Wing* and *Commander in Chief*. But through all that fiction, I keep coming back to the reality of the people who actually held the nation's highest office: who they were, what they did, and how they're remembered.

My passion for the Presidents has been with me from the time my mother, attempting to fill our home with learning experiences, hung a small poster on the wall. The poster had pictures of all the Presidents, along with their names and the dates they served. I memorized that poster. My first political memory is Richard Nixon's resignation, when I was eight. I remember asking my parents if Henry Kissinger was going to be President, since his was the only other political name I knew. They explained to me that we had a Vice President, Gerald Ford, and that he would be the new President. It wasn't long before I understood that, in addition to a Vice President, there was also a Speaker of the House and a President pro tempore of the Senate before we'd look to the Secretary of State. There was also the fact that Kissinger hadn't been born a U.S. citizen.

Well, I was a native-born citizen, so apart from being too young, there was no impediment I could see to being President myself. It wasn't an all-consuming desire; I figured that when the time was right, I'd move in that direction. But in the meantime, I learned more about the Presidents—the people who we'd chosen to represent us to the rest of the world.

As I matured politically, I realized that my views weren't congruent with either of the major parties, which meant becoming President myself was much less likely. That didn't stop me from trying to figure out who these people were who'd made it to the presidency.

The scientific part of my brain wanted to find patterns. Were there some common traits that all the Presidents shared (apart from their citizenship and minimum age) that might point toward who the next would be? Was there some way of knowing ahead of time which candidates were more likely to be chosen? I cast about for books comparing and contrasting the Presidents. While I found a great many books on the Presidents and presidential trivia, I could find none making the correlations I hoped would help me to find the patterns.

So I set about doing the comparisons myself. One led to another, and before I knew it, my agent, Steven Harris, had found a publisher. Jill Schwartzman became my editor, and she and her assistant, Becca Shapiro, enthusiastically supported my efforts.

I still can't tell you who will be the next President based

solely on the forty-two men who've held the office thus far, but I can tell you what the "average" President would look like (see chapter 110, "The Average President"), and the preceding 109 chapters will tell you how I arrived at that.

I hope, like me, you'll be fascinated by just how alike (and how dissimilar) the Presidents are, and also by how much (or how little) you have in common with them.

I haven't completely given up my dreams of being President, but for now, I'm honored to have my name on the cover of this book about them.

A Note on Usage

THE GOVERNMENT HAS DECIDED THAT, IN THE LISTS OF U.S. Presidents, Grover Cleveland is counted as both the 22nd and 24th Presidents, because he served two nonconsecutive terms (he was elected in 1884, lost his bid for reelection in 1888, and then was elected again in 1892). That decree does make it easier to count Presidents and administrations, and that's why, when you see pictures of the two Presidents Bush, the elder's cap says "41" and the younger's "43." Their administrations were the 41st and 43rd. But in this book, which focuses more on the Presidents themselves, and less on their administrations, counting Grover Cleveland as two different people would be inappropriate. Therefore, for our purposes, Grover Cleveland—like each of the other 41 people to hold the nation's highest office—is considered to be one person. And that's why the senior President Bush is the 40th person to hold the office, and the younger is the 42nd.

When it's appropriate to list the Presidents by merely their last names, 32 are unique and present no problem. But five pairs of Presidents shared last names. In those cases, this book uses the following style: JAdams means John Adams (President from 1797 to 1801), JQAdams is John Quincy Adams (1825–29), WHHarrison is William Henry Harrison (1841), AJohnson is Andrew Johnson (1865–69), BHarrison is Benjamin Harrison (1889–93), TRoosevelt is Theodore Roosevelt (1901–09), FDRoosevelt is

Franklin Delano Roosevelt (1933–45), and LBJohnson is Lyndon Baines Johnson (1963–69).

In researching this book, I discovered that there are several methods of determining how closely two people are related. I've decided to use the method advocated by the National Genealogical Society, which seems the most common. In this system, to determine what degree of cousins two people are, count generations back to the common ancestor from each of the two people being compared. Using the person most closely related to the common ancestor, the degree of cousinhood (first, second, etc.) is one less than the number of generations between them. The degree of removedness (once removed, twice removed, etc.) is the number of generations difference between the two people being compared.

Common ancestor	Child	Grandchild	Great-Grandchild	Great-Great-Grandchild	Great(3)-Grandchild
Child	Siblings	Nephew	Grand-Nephew	Great-Nephew	Great-Great-Nephew
Grandchild	Nephew	First Cousins	First Cousins, Once Removed	First Cousins, Twice Removed	First Cousins, Three Times Removed
Great-Grandchild	Grand-· Nephew	First Cousins, Once Removed	Second Cousins	Second Cousins, Once Removed	Second Cousins, Twice Removed
Great-Great-Grandchild	Great-Nephew	First Cousins, Twice Removed	Second Cousins, Once Removed	Third Cousins	Third Cousins, Once Removed
Great(3)-Grandchild	Great-Great-Nephew	First Cousins, Three Times Removed	Second Cousins, Twice Removed	Third Cousins, Once Removed	Fourth Cousins

For example, James Madison and Zachary Taylor shared a pair of great-grandparents, Col. James Taylor and Martha Thompson. Their daughter Frances was President Madison's grandmother, while their son Zachary was President Taylor's grandfather. So we use the box on the left side for "Great-Grandchild" (James Madison) and the box at the top for "Great-Grandchild" (Zachary Taylor), and where those lines intersect, we see that they are second cousins. If, for example, the common ancestors had been Zachary Taylor's great-great-grandparents, we would use that line on the top to find that the two Presidents were second cousins, once removed.

When discussing grandparents and grandchildren, I've used a parenthetical number for more than two greats, for the sake of simplicity. Thus, great(5)-grandparents means great-great-great-great-great-grandparents.

The information in this book is current as of March 1, 2008. For the latest news and updates, read my blog at ianrandalstrock .livejournal.com.

A. General Information List of the Presidents

Name	Birthdate	Birthplace	Presidency	Death Date	Burial Place	Party	Vice President
George Washington	Feb 22, 1732	Westmoreland County, VA	Apr 30, 1789–Mar 4, 1797	Dec 14, 1799	Mt. Vernon, VA	Federalist	John Adams
John Adams	Oct 30, 1735	Quincy, MA	Mar 4, 1797–Mar 4, 1801	Jul 4, 1826	Quincy, MA	Federalist	Thomas Jefferson
Thomas Jefferson	Apr 13, 1743	Albemarle County, VA	Mar 4, 1801–Mar 4, 1809	Jul 4, 1826	Monticello estate, Charlottesville, VA	Democrat-Republican	Aaron Burr / George Clinton
James Madison	Mar 16, 1751	King George County, VA	Mar 4, 1809–Mar 4, 1817	Jun 28, 1836	Montpelier estate, VA	Democrat-Republican	George Clinton / Elbridge Gerry
James Monroe	Apr 28, 1758	Westmoreland County, VA	Mar 4, 1817–Mar 4, 1825	Jul 4, 1831	New York, NY (1831–58); Richmond, VA	Democrat-Republican	Daniel D. Tompkins
John Quincy Adams	Jul 11, 1767	Quincy, MA	Mar 4, 1825–Mar 4, 1829	Feb 23, 1848	Quincy, MA	Democrat-Republican	John C. Calhoun

Name	Birthdate	Birthplace	Presidency	Death Date	Burial Place	Party	Vice President
Andrew Jackson	Mar 15, 1767	Waxhaw, SC	Mar 4, 1829– Mar 4, 1837	Jun 8, 1845	Hermitage estate, Nashville, TN	Democratic	John C. Calhoun / Martin Van Buren
Martin Van Buren	Dec 5, 1782	Kinderhook, NY	Mar 4, 1837– Mar 4, 1841	Jul 24, 1862	Kinderhook, NY	Democratic	Richard M. Johnson
William Henry Harrison	Feb 9, 1773	Charles City County, VA	Mar 4, 1841– Apr 4, 1841	Apr 4, 1841	North Bend, OH	Whig	John Tyler
John Tyler	Mar 29, 1790	Charles City County, VA	Apr 6, 1841– Mar 4, 1845	Jan 18, 1862	Richmond, VA	Whig	
James Knox Polk	Nov 2, 1795	Mecklenburg County, NC	Mar 4, 1845– Mar 4, 1849	Jun 15, 1849	Polk Place, TN (1849–1893); Nashville, TN	Democratic	George M. Dallas
Zachary Taylor	Nov 24, 1784	Orange County, VA	Mar 4, 1849– Jul 9, 1850	Jul 9, 1850	Louisville, KY	Whig	Millard Fillmore
Millard Fillmore	Jan 7, 1800	Locke Township, NY	Jul 10, 1850– Mar 4, 1853	Mar 8, 1874	Buffalo, NY	Whig	

Name	Birthdate	Birthplace	Presidency	Death Date	Burial Place	Party	Vice President
Franklin Pierce	Nov 23, 1804	Hillsborough, NH	Mar 4, 1853–Mar 4, 1857	Oct 8, 1869	Concord, NH	Democratic	William R. King
James Buchanan	Apr 23, 1791	near Cove Gap, PA	Mar 4, 1857–Mar 4, 1861	Jun 1, 1868	Lancaster, PA	Democratic	John C. Breckinridge
Abraham Lincoln	Feb 12, 1809	near Hodgenville, KY	Mar 4, 1861–Apr 15, 1865	Apr 15, 1865	Springfield, IL	Republican	Hannibal Hamlin / Andrew Johnson
Andrew Johnson	Dec 29, 1808	Raleigh, NC	Apr 15, 1865–Mar 4, 1869	Jul 31, 1875	Greeneville, TN	National Union	
Ulysses Simpson Grant	Apr 27, 1822	Port Pleasant, OH	Mar 4, 1869–Mar 4, 1877	Jul 23, 1885	New York, NY	Republican	Schuyler Colfax
Rutherford Birchard Hayes	Oct 4, 1822	Delaware, OH	Mar 4, 1877–Mar 4, 1881	Jan 17, 1893	Oakwood Cemetery, Fremont, OH (1893–1915); Spiegel Grove, Fremont, OH	Republican	William A. Wheeler

Name	Birthdate	Birthplace	Presidency	Death Date	Burial Place	Party	Vice President
James Abram Garfield	Nov 19, 1831	Orange, OH	Mar 4, 1881–Sep 19, 1881	Sep 19, 1881	Cleveland, OH	Republican	Chester Alan Arthur
Chester Alan Arthur	Oct 5, 1829	North Fairfield, VT	Sep 20, 1881–Mar 4, 1885	Nov 18, 1886	Albany, NY	Republican	
Grover Cleveland	Mar 18, 1837	Caldwell, NJ	Mar 4, 1885–Mar 4, 1889; Mar 4, 1893–Mar 4, 1897	Jun 24, 1908	Princeton, NJ	Democratic	Thomas A. Hendricks / Adlai E. Stevenson
Benjamin Harrison	Aug 20, 1833	North Bend, OH	Mar 4, 1889–Mar 4, 1893	Mar 13, 1901	Indianapolis, IN	Republican	Levi P. Morton
William McKinley	Jan 29, 1843	Niles, OH	Mar 4, 1897–Sep 14, 1901	Sep 14, 1901	Westlawn Cemetery, Canton, OH (1901–1907); McKinley National Memorial, Canton, OH	Republican	Garret A. Hobart / Theodore Roosevelt

Name	Birthdate	Birthplace	Presidency	Death Date	Burial Place	Party	Vice President
Theodore Roosevelt	Oct 27, 1858	New York City, NY	Sep 14, 1901–Mar 4, 1909	Jan 6, 1919	Oyster Bay, NY	Republican	Charles W. Fairbanks
William Howard Taft	Sep 15, 1857	Cincinnati, OH	Mar 4, 1909–Mar 4, 1913	Mar 8, 1930	Arlington National Cemetery, VA	Republican	James S. Sherman
Woodrow Wilson	Dec 28, 1856	Staunton, VA	Mar 4, 1913–Mar 4, 1921	Feb 3, 1924	National Cathedral, Washington, D.C.	Democratic	Thomas R. Marshall
Warren Gamaliel Harding	Nov 2, 1865	Corsica, OH	Mar 4, 1921–Aug 2, 1923	Aug 2, 1923	Marion, OH	Republican	Calvin Coolidge
Calvin Coolidge	Jul 4, 1872	Plymouth, VT	Aug 3, 1923–Mar 4, 1929	Jan 5, 1933	Plymouth, VT	Republican	Charles G. Dawes
Herbert Clark Hoover	Aug 10, 1874	West Branch, IA	Mar 4, 1929–Mar 4, 1933	Oct 20, 1964	West Branch, IA	Republican	Charles Curtis

Name	Birthdate	Birthplace	Presidency	Death Date	Burial Place	Party	Vice President
Franklin Delano Roosevelt	Jan 30, 1882	Hyde Park, NY	Mar 4, 1933–Apr 12, 1945	Apr 12, 1945	Hyde Park, NY	Democratic	John Nance Garner / Henry Agard Wallace / Harry S Truman
Harry S Truman	May 8, 1884	Lamar, MO	Apr 12, 1945–Jan 20, 1953	Dec 26, 1972	Truman Library, Independence, MO	Democratic	Alben W. Barkley
Dwight David Eisenhower	Oct 14, 1890	Denison, TX	Jan 20, 1953–Jan 20, 1961	Mar 28, 1969	Abilene, KS	Republican	Richard Milhous Nixon
John Fitzgerald Kennedy	May 29, 1917	Brookline, MA	Jan 20, 1961–Nov 22, 1963	Nov 22, 1963	Arlington National Cemetery, VA	Democratic	Lyndon Baines Johnson
Lyndon Baines Johnson	Aug 27, 1908	near Johnson City, TX	Nov 22, 1963–Jan 20, 1969	Jan 22, 1973	Johnson City, TX	Democratic	Hubert H. Humphrey
Richard Milhous Nixon	Jan 9, 1913	Yorba Linda, CA	Jan 20, 1969–Aug 9, 1974	Apr 22, 1994	Nixon Library and Museum, Yorba Linda, CA	Republican	Spiro T. Agnew / Gerald Rudolph Ford

Name	Birthdate	Birthplace	Presidency	Death Date	Burial Place	Party	Vice President
Gerald Rudolph Ford	Jul 14, 1913	Omaha, NE	Aug 9, 1974– Jan 20, 1977	Dec 26, 2006	Ford Library and Museum, Grand Rapids, MI	Republican	Nelson A. Rockefeller
James Earl "Jimmy" Carter	Oct 1, 1924	Plains, GA	Jan 20, 1977– Jan 20, 1981			Democratic	Walter Mondale
Ronald Wilson Reagan	Feb 6, 1911	Tampico, IL	Jan 20, 1981– Jan 20, 1989	Jun 5, 2004	Reagan Library, Simi Valley, CA	Republican	George H.W. Bush
George H.W. Bush	Jun 12, 1924	Milton, MA	Jan 20, 1989– Jan 20, 1993			Republican	J. Danforth Quayle
William Jefferson Clinton	Aug 19, 1946	Hope, AR	Jan 20, 1993– Jan 20, 2001			Democratic	Al Gore, Jr.
George W. Bush	Jul 6, 1946	New Haven, CT	Jan 20, 2001–			Republican	Richard Bruce Cheney

B. *About Washington's Predecessors*

GEORGE WASHINGTON BECAME THE FIRST PRESIDENT IN 1789, BUT the rebellious colonies declared their independence in 1776. Those two facts beg the question: Who was in charge for those intervening 13 years?

The short answer is: no one.

The somewhat longer answer is that the newly independent United States of America were fighting a war against a seemingly overbearing central authority figure (King George III), and the last thing they wanted was to set up another all-powerful central authority figure. Thus, they kept themselves together as 13 nearly autonomous countries. But following the Declaration of Independence, they realized they needed some form of central government, and the Second Continental Congress wrote the Articles of Confederation. This form of government codified relations among the 13 states, and set up a system of making national decisions (though the decision-making authority was the United States in Congress). The Articles were written in 1777 and ratified in 1781. Under this document, there was no position analogous to the modern President of the United States.

When Congress did meet, they chose a member to serve as President of the United States in Congress ("President" from the word "preside"), so these leaders are as close as we can find to Washington's predecessors: They had none of his authority and none of his power, and though they may have been leaders of the nation, it was merely in the role of a presiding officer in a legislature.

When the Treaty of Paris was signed in 1783, formally ending the Revolutionary War, the new nation could get down to the business of actually being an independent country. It wasn't long before the Federalists realized that the Articles of Confederation weren't an efficient form of government. The Articles gave almost no power to the central government—which was fine for the independent states leery of ceding too much authority to a "king" figure—but those independent states were too small to do many of the things a centralized government can do effectively. So several men—specifically Alexander Hamilton, John Jay, and James Madison—wrote the Federalist Papers, which were designed to convince the citizenry of the need for a more powerful, more centralized government. They worked, and in 1787 the Constitution was written and sent out for ratification. Following its adoption, the office of President of the United States was established, and Washington was elected the first President.

So Washington's predecessors, those who spoke for the United States of America, were the Presidents of the Congress for the United Colonies of America. They were:

PEYTON RANDOLPH (1721–75), of Virginia, President from September 5 to October 21, 1774, was a member of the Virginia House of Burgesses. His nephew, Edmund Randolph, would later be first Attorney General of the United States, and then the nation's second Secretary of State. Third President Thomas Jefferson was Peyton Randolph's first cousin once removed. Chief Justice John Marshall was his first cousin twice removed.

HENRY MIDDLETON (1717–84), of South Carolina, was President from October 22 to 26, 1774. His son Arthur signed the Declaration of Independence. Arthur's son Henry was governor of South

Carolina (1810–12), a member of the House of Representatives (1815–19), and U.S. Minister to Russia (1820–30).

The Second Continental Congress began its work in 1775, and also chose PEYTON RANDOLPH (see above) as its first President. Randolph served May 10–23, 1775. JOHN HANCOCK (1737–93), of Massachusetts, followed Randolph, taking office on May 24, 1775. During Hancock's presidency, the Congress adopted the Declaration of Independence, and Hancock, as President, famously signed it first and largest. Hancock later served as governor of Massachusetts from 1780 to 1785, and again from 1787 to 1793.

HENRY LAURENS (1724–92), of South Carolina, served from November 1, 1777, to December 9, 1778. He had been vice president of South Carolina from March 1776 to June 1777. After serving as President of Congress, he was the U.S. Minister to Holland, taking up that post in 1780. Traveling by ship while on duty, he was taken captive by the British and charged with treason. He was released on December 31, 1781, in exchange for General Lord Cornwallis.

JOHN JAY (1745–1829), of New York, served from December 10, 1778, to September 27, 1779. He was the U.S. Minister Plenipotentiary to Spain from 1779 to 1782, and then became the new country's second Secretary of Foreign Affairs (1784–90), a job he held until Thomas Jefferson returned from France on March 22, 1790, to become the first Secretary of State. Jay was the first Chief Justice of United States, serving from October 19, 1789, to June 29, 1795, when he resigned to become governor of New York (1795–1801).

SAMUEL HUNTINGTON (1731–96), of Connecticut, served from September 28, 1779, to March 1, 1781. He was a signer of the Declaration of Independence, and later served as governor of Connecticut (1786–96). During Huntington's term, the Articles of Confederation came into effect, and the title of his position was changed to President of the United States in Congress Assembled. Huntington held that new post until July 9, 1781.

THOMAS MCKEAN (1734–1817), of Delaware, and later Pennsylvania, served from July 10 to November 4, 1781. He had previously been the president of Delaware (September 22–October 20, 1777), was a Continental Congressman from Delaware twice (August 2, 1774–November 7, 1776, and December 17, 1777–February 1, 1783), was chief justice of Pennsylvania (July 28, 1777–December 17, 1799), and later the state's governor (December 17, 1799–December 20, 1808).

JOHN HANSON (1715–83), of Maryland, served November 5, 1781–November 3, 1782. Hanson represented Maryland in the Continental Congress from 1780 to 1782, and had previously represented Charles County, Maryland, in the Colonial Assembly off and on from 1757 to 1769.

ELIAS BOUDINOT (1740–1821), of New Jersey, served November 4, 1782–November 2, 1783. He represented New Jersey in the House of Representatives during the first three Congresses (1789–95), and was then appointed director of the U.S. Mint, holding that post from October 1795 until 1805.

THOMAS MIFFLIN (1744–1800), of Pennsylvania, served November 3, 1783–October 31, 1784. He was president of Pennsylvania from November 5, 1788, until December 21, 1790, when the title of his office was changed to governor. He finally left that office on December 17, 1799.

RICHARD HENRY LEE (1732–94) of Virginia served November 30, 1784–November 6, 1785. He had signed the Declaration of Independence, and was later a senator representing Virginia

(1789–92). While in the Senate, he served as President pro tempore from April 18 to October 8, 1792.

JOHN HANCOCK of Massachusetts (see above) returned to the presidency on November 23, 1785. Though he held the title until June 5, 1786, his failing health prevented him from actually doing the job, so two others acted in his stead: DAVID RAMSAY (1749–1815), of South Carolina (until May 12, 1786), and then NATHANIEL GORHAM (1738–96), of Massachusetts. Gorham then succeeded Hancock, and was President in his own right from June 6 until November 5, 1786.

ARTHUR ST. CLAIR was born in Scotland and immigrated to Pennsylvania in 1764. He served as President from February 2 to November 4, 1787. After his service, he was appointed the governor of the Northwest Territory (which included the land that would later become Ohio, Indiana, Illinois, and Michigan, as well as parts of Wisconsin and Minnesota) from its formation in 1787 until it was divided in 1800, when he became governor of the Ohio Territory. He was removed from office in 1802.

CYRUS GRIFFIN (1749–1810), of Virginia, was the last President of the United States in Congress Assembled, serving from January 22, 1788, until March 2, 1789.

ONE

LIFE AND DEATH

The Five Presidents Who Lived Longest

1. GERALD FORD. Born on July 14, 1913, he overtook Ronald Reagan as the oldest President on November 12, 2006, and then died December 26, 2006. He was 93 years, 164 days old.

2. RONALD REAGAN. Born on February 6, 1911, he was 93 years, 120 days old when he died on June 5, 2004. In October 2001 he eclipsed John Adams's record, which had stood since 1826.

3. JOHN ADAMS. Born on October 30, 1735, more than 40 years before the United States itself was born, our second President was the longest lived for almost two centuries. He took the title from George Washington in 1802, and held it until 2001. He died on July 4, 1826, aged 90 years, 247 days.

4. HERBERT HOOVER. Born on August 10, 1874, he lived 90 years, 71 days, and died on October 20, 1964, having been retired from the presidency for 31 years.

5. HARRY TRUMAN. Born May 8, 1884, he was 88 years, 232 days old when he died on December 26, 1972.

Only four Presidents have held the title of "longest lived": George Washington (who, as the first President, held most of the titles first), John Adams, Ronald Reagan, and Gerald Ford.

George H.W. Bush won't be able to knock Truman off this list until January 30, 2013 (he'll take the title from Ford on November 24, 2017). Jimmy Carter is 111 days younger than GHWBush. George W. Bush will be 88 years, 232 days old on February 23, 2039. Bill Clinton is 41 days younger than his successor, GWBush.

2

The Five Presidents Who Died Youngest

1. JOHN F. KENNEDY. The youngest to be elected was also the youngest to die. He was assassinated in his third year in office, on November 22, 1963, at the age of 46 years, 177 days.

2. JAMES A. GARFIELD. The second President to be assassinated, he was shot on July 2, 1881, but lingered another two months, before succumbing on September 19 at the age of 49 years, 304 days.

3. JAMES K. POLK. The shortest-lived President to not die in office, Polk served one term (1845–49) and then died three months after leaving office, on June 15, 1849, aged 53 years, 225 days.

4. ABRAHAM LINCOLN. The first to be assassinated, he was 56 years, 64 days old when he died on April 15, 1865, a day after John Wilkes Booth shot him.

5. CHESTER A. ARTHUR. He succeeded to the presidency upon Garfield's death (see above), served out the term, and then died a year and a half after leaving office, on November 18, 1886, aged 57 years, 44 days.

All four living Presidents (Carter, both Bushes, and Clinton) are already ineligible for this list.

Splitting the list into those who died in office and those who died after retiring, we get:

The five Presidents who died the youngest while in office:

1. JOHN F. KENNEDY (see above).

2. JAMES A. GARFIELD (see above).

3. ABRAHAM LINCOLN (see above).

4. WARREN G. HARDING. He died in office on August 2, 1923, aged 57 years, 273 days.

5. WILLIAM McKINLEY. Shot September 6, 1901, died September 14, aged 58 years, 228 days.

George W. Bush became ineligible for this list on February 19, 2005.

The five Presidents who died the youngest after leaving office:

1. JAMES K. POLK (see above).

2. CHESTER A. ARTHUR (see above).

3. THEODORE ROOSEVELT. He died after serving his seven years and then running unsuccessfully against his successor, William H. Taft, in 1912. He died January 6, 1919, aged 60 years, 71 days.

4. CALVIN COOLIDGE. He served the end of Harding's term and then was elected for a term of his own. He died on January 5, 1933, aged 60 years, 185 days.

5. ULYSSES S. GRANT. After a hard-drinking life, he died on July 23, 1885, aged 63 years, 87 days.

Franklin D. Roosevelt does not appear on either of these lists. He died younger than Grant (63 years, 72 days), but he died in office.

Presidents Carter and George H.W. Bush are already ineligible for these lists. Bill Clinton will be 63 years, 87 days old on November 14, 2009. His successor, George W. Bush, will be that old on October 1, 2009.

3

The Five Presidents Who Died Soonest After Leaving Office

SOME RETIRED PRESIDENTS ARE RESPECTED, OTHERS CAN LIVE TO see bad reputations slowly mollified, but these Presidents had very little time to enjoy their retirements.

1. JAMES KNOX POLK. He chose not to run for reelection in 1848, and retired from his one term on March 4, 1849. He died 103 days later, on June 15.

2. CHESTER A. ARTHUR. He became President upon Garfield's death, but lost his bid to be nominated for his own term in 1884, and died one year, 259 days after leaving office, on November 18, 1886.

3. GEORGE WASHINGTON. The first President was the only President to leave office in the 1700s, and the only President to die in the 1700s. He died on December 14, 1799, two years, 285 days after leaving office.

4. WOODROW WILSON. He suffered a stroke while President, and some rumors say he was so incapacitated by it that his wife was acting President for the final five months of his presidency. Nevertheless, he survived another two years, 335 days after leaving office, dying on February 3, 1924.

5. CALVIN COOLIDGE. He refused to be renominated for another term in 1928, and retired after six years in office. He died on January 5, 1933, three years, 337 days after leaving office.

6. LYNDON B. JOHNSON. He refused to be renominated for another term in 1968, and retired after five years in office. He died on January 22, 1973, four years, two days after leaving office. He doesn't fit into the top five, but misses the list by a scant 31 days.

In order for George W. Bush to avoid a place on this list, he'll have to survive until January 22, 2013, at which time he'll be 66 years old.

4

The Five Presidents Who Lived Longest After Leaving Office

1. HERBERT HOOVER. After serving one term, which saw the beginning of the Great Depression, Hoover lost his bid for reelection in 1932, and after Franklin Delano Roosevelt's inauguration in 1933, he lived for 31 years, 230 days as a retired President, serving the government in several appointed positions before his death in 1964.

2. GERALD FORD. After succeeding to office following Richard Nixon's resignation, Ford's pardoning of Nixon may have guaranteed his loss in the election of 1976. He left office on January 20, 1977, and upon his death on December 26, 2006, had been retired for 29 years, 340 days.

3. JIMMY CARTER. The 39th President, also served only one term, losing his bid for reelection. He left office on January 20, 1981, four years after Gerald Ford, and passed John Adams (see next entry) on May 22, 2006. He'll pass Ford on December 27, 2010, and Hoover on September 7, 2012.

4. JOHN ADAMS. The second President served only one term, and was the second President to die, but between his retirement on March 4, 1801 (when Thomas Jefferson was inaugurated), and his death on July 4, 1826 (the same day as Jefferson), he was retired for 25 years, 122 days.

5. MARTIN VAN BUREN. After losing the election of 1840 to the then-oldest President, William Henry Harrison, Van Buren was almost nominated for President in 1844, and then ran for President on the Free Soil ticket in 1848. When he died on July 24, 1862, he'd been retired for 21 years, 142 days.

George H.W. Bush will pass Millard Fillmore (sixth on the list at 21 years, four days) on January 24, 2014, and Van Buren on June 11 of the same year (which will be the day before his 90th birthday).

Bill Clinton is precisely eight years behind GHWBush, and will pass Van Buren on June 11, 2022, two months before his 76th birthday.

George W. Bush will be precisely eight years behind Clinton, and will pass Van Buren on June 11, 2030, one month before his 84th birthday.

5

The Five Tallest Presidents

THERE HAVE BEEN STORIES THAT THE TALLER PRESIDENTIAL CAN-
didate always wins, or that added height gives one added respect.
The former is not necessarily so. In the elections in which the
heights of both major candidates were known, the taller candidate won less than 60 percent of the time. But does height lend
greatness? Only history can judge.

The tallest Presidents were:

1. ABRAHAM LINCOLN 6′4″. Did his height bring him greatness, or
was it the time in which he lived and the challenges he faced?
Lincoln was President during the Civil War, and the first to be
assassinated.

2. LYNDON BAINES JOHNSON 6′3″. He succeeded to the presidency
upon the assassination of John Kennedy, then went on to be
elected to his own term in 1964, and chose not to run for reelection in 1968.

3 (tie). THOMAS JEFFERSON 6′2.5″. The third President wrote the
Declaration of Independence, presided over the Louisiana Purchase, and is known for great achievements in a wide variety of
fields.

3 (tie). BILL CLINTON 6'2.5". The first Democrat to be reelected since Franklin Roosevelt, Clinton was only the second President to be impeached (following Andrew Johnson). Like Johnson, he was acquitted.

5 (tie). GEORGE WASHINGTON 6'2". Commander of the Continental Army and later the first President, he would have been known as a terrorist or a rebel had England been able to retain their upstart American colonies.

5 (tie). CHESTER ALAN ARTHUR 6'2". He succeeded to the presidency when assassinated President James Garfield died in late 1881, but was not nominated for his own term in 1884, and retired in 1885, only to die a year later.

5 (tie). WILLIAM HOWARD TAFT 6'2". He was Theodore Roosevelt's handpicked successor, and served one term, 1909–13. He lost his bid for reelection when Roosevelt challenged him in the election of 1912, giving Woodrow Wilson the election. In 1921, President Warren Harding appointed Taft Chief Justice of the Supreme Court, the position he'd most ardently desired all his life. He served as Chief Justice until early 1930, retiring for health reasons about a month before he died.

5 (tie). GEORGE H.W. BUSH 6'2". He was the first sitting Vice President to be elected President since Martin Van Buren did it in 1836. Like Van Buren, he served only one term, and then was defeated in his bid for reelection. In 2000 he became only the second President to see his son also elected President.

6

The Five Shortest Presidents

AS THE PREVIOUS CHAPTER STATES, DESPITE CONVENTIONAL WIS-dom, the taller candidate wins only 60 percent of the time. Two of the four tallest Presidents were elected in the second half of the 20th century. But of the shortest Presidents, the latest to serve was elected in 1900. Is height a requirement in the media age? Only history can judge.

1. JAMES MADISON 5′4″. The fourth President nearly single-handedly wrote the Constitution. He's also famous for his viva-cious wife, Dolley, who acted as White House hostess for Madison's predecessor, widower Thomas Jefferson. The third of the four Presidents known as the "Virginia Dynasty"—Washing-ton, Jefferson, Madison, and Monroe—he's the only one on this list (Washington and Jefferson are both on the list of the tallest).

2 (tie). JOHN ADAMS 5′6″. The first Vice President of the United States was elected the second President when Washington re-tired, but he only served one term before being defeated by Thomas Jefferson. He was also the longest-lived President (he lived 90 years) until Ronald Reagan exceeded his longevity record in 2001.

2 (tie). MARTIN VAN BUREN 5'6". The ninth President (he served 1837–41) was the last sitting Vice President to be elected President until George H.W. Bush did it in 1988.

2 (tie). BENJAMIN HARRISON 5'6". The only grandson of a President to be elected President, he served only one term. He defeated sitting President Grover Cleveland in the election of 1888, and then lost when Cleveland came back to beat him in the election of 1892.

5 (tie). ULYSSES S. GRANT 5'7". The general who won the Civil War was only 5'1" when he entered West Point (he made the height requirement by a scant inch), but shot up to 5'7" by the time he graduated. The man he served during the war, Lincoln, was the tallest President.

5 (tie). WILLIAM McKINLEY 5'7". The last President elected in the 19th century, and the first to serve in the 20th, he was assassinated at the Pan American Exposition in Buffalo, New York, and is frequently overshadowed by the Vice President who succeeded him, Theodore Roosevelt.

7

Most Common Presidential First Names

1. JAMES was shared by six Presidents: MADISON, MONROE, POLK, BUCHANAN, GARFIELD, and CARTER.

2. JOHN was shared by five Presidents: both ADAMSES, TYLER, and KENNEDY. Although COOLIDGE went by the name Calvin, his given name was John.

3. WILLIAM was shared by four Presidents: the first HARRISON, MCKINLEY, TAFT, and CLINTON (although he was commonly known as Bill).

4. GEORGE was shared by three Presidents: WASHINGTON and both BUSHES.

5 (tie). ANDREW: JACKSON and the first JOHNSON.

5 (tie). FRANKLIN: PIERCE and the second ROOSEVELT.

5 (tie). THOMAS: JEFFERSON and WILSON (although Wilson went by Woodrow).

The first President to have a unique first name is eighth President Martin Van Buren.

8

Most Popular States Where Presidents Were Born

SEVEN STATES ACCOUNT FOR 29 OF THE 42 PRESIDENTS—A REmarkably concentrated pattern of births—and only 20 states can lay claim to at least one Presidential birth. Of the original 13 states, Delaware, Maryland, and Rhode Island have still not produced Presidents.

1. Virginia was the birthplace for eight of the Presidents, including four of the first six (sometimes called the Virginia Dynasty): GEORGE WASHINGTON (born in 1732), THOMAS JEFFERSON (1743), JAMES MADISON (1751), JAMES MONROE (1758), WILLIAM HENRY

HARRISON (1773), ZACHARY TAYLOR (1784), JOHN TYLER (1790), and WOODROW WILSON (1856).

2. In a span of 43 years, Ohio gave birth to seven Presidents (including the grandson of one of the Virginians): ULYSSES GRANT (1822), RUTHERFORD B. HAYES (1822), JAMES A. GARFIELD (1831), BENJAMIN HARRISON (1833), WILLIAM MCKINLEY (1843), WILLIAM HOWARD TAFT (1857), and WARREN G. HARDING (1865).

3 (tie). Massachusetts birthed the two non-Virginians of the original six, but then became less prolific. The Bay State now claims four Presidents as native sons: JOHN ADAMS (1735), JOHN QUINCY ADAMS (1767), JOHN F. KENNEDY (1917), and GEORGE H.W. BUSH (1924).

3 (tie). New York also lays claim to four Presidents: MARTIN VAN BUREN (1782), MILLARD FILLMORE (1800), THEODORE ROOSEVELT (1858), and FRANKLIN DELANO ROOSEVELT (1882).

5 (tie). North Carolina: JAMES KNOX POLK (1795) and ANDREW JOHNSON (1808).

5 (tie). Vermont: CHESTER ALAN ARTHUR (1829) and CALVIN COOLIDGE (1872). Arthur may actually have been born in Canada, since his parents lived there for a time. If that's true, he would have been ineligible to be President. His birthplace is generally accepted as Vermont.

5 (tie). Texas: DWIGHT DAVID EISENHOWER (1890) and LYNDON BAINES JOHNSON (1908).

Presidents Born Outside the Original 13 Colonies

The Presidents born outside the original 13 states include the entire Ohio contingent (see above), as well as the two from Vermont (see above), and from Texas (see above), and the following, who were each the only son of their state to make it to the White House: Abraham Lincoln (Kentucky, 1809), Herbert Hoover (Iowa, 1874), Harry Truman (Missouri, 1884), Ronald Reagan (Illinois, 1911), Richard Nixon (California, 1913), Gerald Ford (Nebraska, 1913), and Bill Clinton (Arkansas, 1946).

9

Presidents Born Outside the United States

THE PRESIDENTS BORN BEFORE THE UNITED STATES BECAME INDE-pendent were technically born in another country; in all cases, England. These include: George Washington (1732), John Adams (1735), Thomas Jefferson (1743), James Madison (1751), James Monroe (1758), Andrew Jackson (1767), John Quincy Adams (1767), and William Henry Harrison (1773).

To this list we may add Chester Alan Arthur, who was born in 1829: He might actually have been born in Canada. His parents were residents of Vermont, and until recently that state was always claimed as Arthur's birthplace. But new research indicates that his parents might have lived for a time—the time of Chester's birth—in Canada. If this new data turns out to be true, President Arthur would be the only one to be ineligible to serve (by dint of his not being a native-born U.S. citizen). How-ever, since there was no debate on the issue at the time of his service, and since he's been dead since 1886, the point is at best moot.

10

Most Popular States Where Presidents Were Buried

1. Virginia is the final resting place of the greatest number of Presidents, which may not be surprising, since it's also the birthplace of the greatest number. However, the seven who are buried there were not all born in the state. In Virginia, one can see the graves of: GEORGE WASHINGTON (died 1799), THOMAS JEFFERSON (1826), JAMES MONROE (1831), JAMES MADISON (1836), JOHN TYLER (1862), WILLIAM HOWARD TAFT (1930, born in Ohio), and JOHN F. KENNEDY (1963, born in Massachusetts).

2. New York is the burial place of six Presidents (including the four born there): MARTIN VAN BUREN (1862), MILLARD FILLMORE (1874), ULYSSES GRANT (1885, born in Ohio), CHESTER ARTHUR (1886, born in Vermont), THEODORE ROOSEVELT (1919), and FRANKLIN DELANO ROOSEVELT (1945).

3. Ohio, birth state of seven Presidents, is burial state to five, including four native sons: WILLIAM HENRY HARRISON (1841, born in Virginia), JAMES A. GARFIELD (1881), RUTHERFORD B. HAYES (1893), WILLIAM MCKINLEY (1901), and WARREN G. HARDING (1923).

4. Tennessee, birthplace of no Presidents, became the home, and then the final resting place, of three: ANDREW JACKSON (1845,

born in South Carolina), JAMES K. POLK (1849, born in North Carolina), and ANDREW JOHNSON (1875, born in North Carolina).

5 (tie). Massachusetts. Of the four born in the state, one is buried in Arlington National Cemetery and one is still alive, leaving only two, who are buried in the same church, father and son: JOHN ADAMS (1826) and JOHN QUINCY ADAMS (1848).

5 (tie). California. Two of the three Presidents who died most recently called California home, and chose it for their burial sites: RICHARD NIXON (1994) and RONALD REAGAN (2004, born in Illinois).

The President Buried in Washington, D.C.

When it was designed and being built, one of the thoughts about the National Cathedral, in Washington, D.C., was that it would become an American Westminster Abbey, a place where the Presidents would be buried. But in the last few decades, as Presidents have opened libraries and museums dedicated to their lives and careers, those memorials have also been planned as their final resting places. As a result, only one President is buried in Washington, D.C. (in the Cathedral): Woodrow Wilson.

Presidents Buried in Arlington National Cemetery

Two Presidents are buried in Arlington National Cemetery.

Former President and then recently retired Chief Justice William Howard Taft was buried there in 1930.

In 1963, recently assassinated President John F. Kennedy was buried under an eternal flame. Later, Kennedy's assassinated brother, Senator and presidential candidate Robert F. Kennedy (who had been Attorney General during his brother's administration), was buried with him.

The First and Last Presidents Born in the 1700s, 1800s, and 1900s

FIRST TO BE BORN IN THE 1700S — FIRST TO BE BORN AT ALL — WAS George Washington (1789–97). He was born on February 22, 1732 (although at the time it was called February 11: England and the colonies hadn't yet switched over to the Gregorian calendar), more than 44 years before the Declaration of Independence was written.

Eleventh President James Knox Polk (1845–49) was the last President to be born in the 1700s, on November 2, 1795, although James Buchanan (1857–61), the 15th President, was the last child of the 1700s to be elected (he was born April 23, 1791, before his two predecessors).

Millard Fillmore, the 13th President (1850–53), was the first to be born in the 1800s (although the last who was born in the 17th century), on January 7, 1800.

The last child of the 1800s to serve as President, Dwight David Eisenhower (1953–61), was born October 14, 1890.

The first 1900s baby to be elected President was John Fitzgerald Kennedy (1961–63), Eisenhower's successor. He was born May 29, 1917. His successor, Lyndon Baines Johnson, was the President born earliest in the 1900s (August 27,

1908). Kennedy successors Richard Nixon, Gerald Ford, and Ronald Reagan were also born earlier in the 20th century than Kennedy.

12

The First and Last Presidents to Die in the 1700s, 1800s, 1900s, and 2000s

ONCE AGAIN, GEORGE WASHINGTON IS THE FIRST. IN THIS CASE, the only. The only President to die in the 1700s, he died December 14, 1799, aged 67, less than three years after leaving office.

The first Presidents to die in the 1800s are pretty much a tie. Second and third Presidents John Adams (1797–1801) and Thomas Jefferson (1801–09) died within hours of each other on July 4, 1826, the 50th anniversary of the Declaration of Independence. Adams, aged 90, was the longest-lived President for the next 175 years, until Ronald Reagan passed him.

The last presidential death in the 19th century was that of 19th President Rutherford Birchard Hayes (1877–81), who died on January 17, 1893. He outlived his two successors, James Garfield, who was assassinated in 1881, and Chester Arthur, who died in 1886.

The first presidential funeral in the 20th century was for 23rd President Benjamin Harrison (1889–93), who died on March 13, 1901. Six months later, William McKinley was assassinated.

The last presidential funeral of the 20th century was for 37th

President Richard Milhous Nixon (1969–74), who died April 22, 1994.

The first presidential funeral in the 21st century was for 40th President Ronald Wilson Reagan (1981–89), who died on June 5, 2004, aged 93, the longest-lived President (he took that title away from John Adams in 2001). However, 38th President Gerald Ford (1974–77), who was two years younger than Reagan, was the first President to survive into the 21st century. He died on December 26, 2006, having taken the longest-lived title from Reagan 44 days before his death.

13

Presidents Who Shared Birthdays

JAMES KNOX POLK (1795) AND WARREN GAMALIEL HARDING (1865) were both born on November 2. They were the only Presidents to share a birthday.

However, several pairs missed sharing a birthday by one day:

WILLIAM MCKINLEY (January 29, 1843) and FRANKLIN DELANO ROOSEVELT (January 30, 1882).

ANDREW JACKSON (March 15, 1767) and JAMES MADISON (March 16, 1751).

ULYSSES S. GRANT (April 27, 1822) and JAMES MONROE (April 28, 1758).

RUTHERFORD B. HAYES (October 4, 1822) and CHESTER A. ARTHUR (October 5, 1830).

FRANKLIN PIERCE (November 23, 1804) and ZACHARY TAYLOR (November 24, 1784).

WOODROW WILSON (December 28, 1856) and ANDREW JOHNSON (December 29, 1808).

14

Presidents Who Shared Death Days

March 8: MILLARD FILLMORE (1874) and WILLIAM HOWARD TAFT (1930).

July 4: Second President JOHN ADAMS and third President THOMAS JEFFERSON died within hours of each other on July 4, 1826, the 50th anniversary of the signing of the Declaration of Independence. Fifth President JAMES MONROE followed them on July 4, 1831.

December 26: HARRY TRUMAN (1972) and GERALD FORD (2006).

Several pairs missed sharing a death day by one day:

CALVIN COOLIDGE (January 5, 1933) and THEODORE ROOSEVELT (January 6, 1919).

RUTHERFORD B. HAYES (January 17, 1893) and JOHN TYLER (January 18, 1862).

ULYSSES S. GRANT (July 23, 1885) and MARTIN VAN BUREN (July 24, 1862).

Presidents Who Shared Last Names with Vice Presidents (Who Did Not Later Become President)

THREE VICE PRESIDENTS HAD PRESIDENTIAL FAMILY NAMES BUT never were President. All of them served before the Presidents who shared their names.

George Clinton became Vice President when Thomas Jefferson won his second term as President, taking office March 4, 1805, and continued in the office as James Madison was elected. Clinton died in office on April 20, 1812. He shares his family name with Bill Clinton, who was President from 1993 to 2001.

Richard M. Johnson was Martin Van Buren's Vice President, serving from 1837 to 1841. He shares his family name with two unrelated Presidents, Andrew Johnson (1865–69) and Lyndon Baines Johnson (1963–69), both of whom were Vice Presidents who succeeded to the presidency upon the death of their predecessors.

After a scandal during President Grant's first term, Vice President Schuyler Colfax was denied renomination. In his place, Senator Henry Wilson was nominated, and won election as President Grant was handily reelected. Vice President Wilson took office on March 4, 1873, and then suffered two strokes. He died in office on November 22, 1875. He shared his name with later President Woodrow Wilson (1913–21).

The Presidents Who Outlived the Greatest Number of Their Successors

1. MARTIN VAN BUREN, whose 25 years of retirement places him fifth on that list, outlived four of his successors. He served as President from 1837 to 1841, and died July 24, 1862. Before his death, he saw the deaths of William Henry Harrison (April 4, 1841, in office), James Knox Polk (June 15, 1849, six months after his retirement from the office), Zachary Taylor (July 9, 1850, in office), and John Tyler (January 18, 1862, who had succeeded Harrison and served the term of 1841–45).

2. MILLARD FILLMORE outlived three of his successors. After serving from 1850 to 1853, he lived another 21 years, dying March 8, 1874. He outlived his three immediate successors: Franklin Pierce (who died October 8, 1869), James Buchanan (June 1, 1868), and Abraham Lincoln (assassinated April 15, 1865).

Eight Presidents lived long enough to see two of their successors predecease them: John Quincy Adams (who saw the deaths of Andrew Jackson and William Henry Harrison), John Tyler (James Knox Polk and Zachary Taylor), Franklin Pierce (James Buchanan and Abraham Lincoln), Rutherford B. Hayes (James Abram Garfield and Chester Alan Arthur), Grover

Cleveland (Benjamin Harrison and William McKinley), William Howard Taft (Woodrow Wilson and Warren G. Harding), Herbert Hoover (Franklin Delano Roosevelt and John Fitzgerald Kennedy), and Harry S. Truman (Dwight David Eisenhower and John Fitzgerald Kennedy). Hoover, who was retired from the Presidency 31 years—longer than any other President—outlived only two of his successors, both of whom died in office.

17

Presidents Older Than the Greatest Number of Their Predecessors

1. RONALD WILSON REAGAN. Born February 6, 1911, he was the oldest when he became President, the oldest President to retire, and, for a few years, the longest-lived President. He was also older than four of his predecessors when he became President in 1981: John Fitzgerald Kennedy (born May 29, 1917, served 1960–63), Richard M. Nixon (born January 9, 1913, served 1969–74), Gerald R. Ford (born July 14, 1913, served 1974–77), and Jimmy Carter (born October 1, 1924, served 1977–81). He outlived Kennedy (who was assassinated in office) and Nixon (who died in 1994, ten years before Reagan).

2. JAMES BUCHANAN, who was born April 23, 1791—and was two months shy of his 66th birthday when he became President in 1857—was older than three of his predecessors: James Knox Polk (born November 2, 1795, served 1845–49), Millard Fillmore

(born January 7, 1800, served 1850–53), and Franklin Pierce (born November 23, 1804, served 1853–57).

3 (tie). ZACHARY TAYLOR, born November 24, 1784, was older than his two immediate predecessors when he became President in 1849: John Tyler (born March 29, 1790, served 1841–45) and James Knox Polk (born November 2, 1795, served 1845–49).

3 (tie). WOODROW WILSON (1913–21) was born December 28, 1856, and was just a little bit older than his two immediate predecessors. They were Theodore Roosevelt (born October 27, 1858, served 1901–09) and William Howard Taft (born September 15, 1857, served 1909–13).

18

Presidents Who Had No Living Predecessors

1. GEORGE WASHINGTON. As the first President, he had no predecessors at all.

2. JOHN ADAMS, from December 14, 1799, when George Washington died, until he left office March 4, 1801.

3. THEODORE ROOSEVELT, from Grover Cleveland's death, June 24, 1908, until he left office March 4, 1909.

4. RICHARD NIXON, from Lyndon Johnson's death, January 22, 1973, until he resigned August 9, 1973.

Presidents Who Had the Most Living Predecessors

Three Presidents are tied with five:

ABRAHAM LINCOLN (for 320 days). Martin Van Buren, John Tyler, Millard Fillmore, Franklin Pierce, and James Buchanan were all alive at his inauguration on March 4, 1861. Tyler died January 18, 1862; Van Buren died later the same year, while Fillmore, Pierce, and Buchanan all outlived Lincoln.

BILL CLINTON (for one year, 92 days). Richard Nixon, Gerald Ford, Jimmy Carter, Ronald Reagan, and George H.W. Bush were all alive at his inauguration on January 20, 1993. Nixon died April 22, 1994.

GEORGE W. BUSH (for three years, 137 days). Gerald Ford, Jimmy Carter, Ronald Reagan, George H.W. Bush, and Bill Clinton were all alive at his inauguration on January 20, 2001. Reagan died June 5, 2004.

Time Periods When the Most Former and Current Presidents Were Alive

THERE WERE THREE PERIODS IN U.S. HISTORY WHEN SIX FORMER and current Presidents were alive.

1. March 4, 1861, to January 18, 1862. From ABRAHAM LINCOLN'S inauguration until JOHN TYLER (1841–45) died. Also alive were MARTIN VAN BUREN (1837–41), MILLARD FILLMORE (1850–53), FRANKLIN PIERCE (1853–57), and JAMES BUCHANAN (1857–61).

2. January 20, 1993, to April 22, 1994. From BILL CLINTON'S inauguration until the death of RICHARD NIXON (1969–74). Also alive were GERALD FORD (1974–77), JIMMY CARTER (1977–81), RONALD REAGAN (1981–89), and GEORGE H.W. BUSH (1989–93).

3. January 20, 2001, to June 5, 2004. From GEORGE W. BUSH'S inauguration until the death of RONALD REAGAN (1981–89). Also alive were GERALD FORD (1974–77), JIMMY CARTER (1977–81), GEORGE H.W. BUSH (1989–93), and BILL CLINTON (1993–2001).

The first time there were five living former and current Presidents was from the inauguration of JOHN QUINCY ADAMS (March 4, 1825) until the deaths of his father, John Adams, and Thomas Jefferson, who both died on July 4, 1826.

Since then there have been six other times when there were five living Presidents: March 4–June 8, 1845 (Polk's inauguration to Jackson's death), March 4, 1857–March 4, 1861 (Buchanan's entire term of office), January 18–July 24, 1862 (Tyler's death to Van Buren's death), January 20, 1989–January 20, 1993 (GHW-Bush's term of office), April 22, 1994–January 20, 2001 (Nixon's death until Clinton's retirement), and June 5, 2004–December 26, 2006 (Reagan's death to Ford's death).

21

Years When the Greatest Number of Presidents Were Born

FIVE SEPARATE YEARS SAW THE BIRTHS OF TWO PRESIDENTS EACH:

1767: JOHN QUINCY ADAMS (July 11) and his successor, ANDREW JACKSON (March 15).

1822: ULYSSES SIMPSON GRANT (April 27) and his successor, RUTHERFORD BIRCHARD HAYES (October 4).

1913: RICHARD M. NIXON (January 9) and his successor, GERALD R. FORD (July 14).

1924: JIMMY CARTER (October 1) and GEORGE H.W. BUSH (June 12). They're the only pair of Presidents sharing a birth year who aren't immediate predecessor/successor; Ronald Reagan (born 1911) was President between their terms of office.

1946: BILL CLINTON (August 19) and his successor, GEORGE W. BUSH (July 6).

Years When the Greatest Number of Presidents Died

THREE SEPARATE YEARS SAW THE DEATHS OF TWO PRESIDENTS EACH:

1826: Second and third Presidents JOHN ADAMS and THOMAS JEF-FERSON died within hours of each other on the 50th anniversary of the Declaration of Independence, July 4, 1826.

1862: MARTIN VAN BUREN (1837–41) died July 24, and JOHN TYLER (1841–45) died January 18.

1901: BENJAMIN HARRISON (1889–93) died March 13, and WILLIAM McKINLEY (1897–1901) was assassinated September 14.

Terms of Office When the Greatest Number of Presidents Died

THREE PRESIDENTS HAVE SEEN THREE OF THEIR PREDECESSORS DIE during their terms of office:

1. ULYSSES GRANT. During his eight-year term in the White House (1869–77), Franklin Pierce (1853–57) died on October 8, 1869, Millard Fillmore (1850–53) died on March 8, 1874, and Andrew Johnson (1865–69) died on July 31, 1875.

2. RICHARD NIXON. During his five and a half years in the White House (1969–74), he saw three presidential deaths: Dwight Eisenhower (1953–61) died on March 28, 1969, Harry Truman (1945–53) died on December 26, 1972, and Lyndon Baines Johnson (1963–69) died on January 22, 1973.

3. ABRAHAM LINCOLN's four years as President, 1861–65, also saw three presidential deaths, but the third was his own, on April 15, 1865. Predeceasing him during those years were: John Tyler (1841–45), who died on January 18, 1862; and Martin Van Buren (1837–41), who died on July 24, 1862.

Six other Presidents served during the deaths of two former Presidents: John Quincy Adams (John Adams and Thomas Jefferson), Andrew Jackson (James Monroe and James Madison), James Knox Polk (Andrew Jackson and John Quincy Adams), Grover Cleveland (Ulysses Grant and Chester Arthur), Herbert Hoover (William Howard Taft and Calvin Coolidge), and George W. Bush (Ronald Reagan and Gerald Ford).

Interestingly, during the term of office of the longest-serving President, Franklin Delano Roosevelt, no other Presidents died.

24

Longest Periods During Which No Presidents Died

SEVEN TIMES THERE HAVE BEEN RESPITES OF MORE THAN TEN years between presidential deaths.

1. December 14, 1799, to July 4, 1826; 26 years, 202 days. The time between the first presidential death (GEORGE WASHINGTON) and the second and third (JOHN ADAMS and THOMAS JEFFERSON died on the same day) was the longest period in U.S. history during which no Presidents died.

2. January 22, 1973, to April 22, 1994; 21 years, 90 days. The time between the deaths of LYNDON BAINES JOHNSON and his immediate successor, RICHARD NIXON, both of whom served one full and one partial term of office (Johnson succeeding on Kennedy's assassination; Nixon resigning) was more than two decades.

3. April 12, 1945, to November 22, 1963; 18 years, 224 days. FRANKLIN DELANO ROOSEVELT and JOHN FITZGERALD KENNEDY both died in office, 18 years apart.

4. March 8, 1930, to April 12, 1945; 15 years, 35 days. WILLIAM HOWARD TAFT died after having served four years as President, eight years in retirement, and then ten years as Chief Justice. Fifteen years later, FRANKLIN DELANO ROOSEVELT died at the beginning of his 13th year as President.

5. July 9, 1850, to January 18, 1862; 11 years, 193 days. ZACHARY TAYLOR, who died in office, was the last presidential death for more than a decade, until JOHN TYLER, who left office four years before Taylor was elected, died.

6. June 24, 1908, to January 5, 1919; ten years, 195 days. From the death of GROVER CLEVELAND to the death of THEODORE ROOSEVELT.

7. April 22, 1994, to June 5, 2004; ten years, 44 days. From the death of RICHARD NIXON to that of RONALD REAGAN.

Franklin Delano Roosevelt (numbers 3 and 4, above) and Richard Nixon (numbers 2 and 7) both appear twice on this list. If Roosevelt's death is ignored, the gap between Taft and Kennedy was 33 years, 259 days. If Nixon's death is ignored, the gap between Johnson and Reagan is 31 years, 135 days.

25

The Four Presidents Who Were Assassinated

THE PRESIDENT OF THE UNITED STATES IS THE MOST VISIBLE REPresentative of the nation and of the government. This position engenders great love and great hatred. When considered in those terms, it's almost surprising that only four of the 42 have been assassinated (though there have been other, unsuccessful attempts).

ABRAHAM LINCOLN

On the night of April 14, 1865, five days after Robert E. Lee signed the surrender of Confederate forces at Appomattox to end the Civil War, President Lincoln, his wife, Major Henry Rathbone, and Miss Clara Harris were in the presidential box at Ford's Theater to see a performance of *Our American Cousin*. At 10:15 that night, 27-year-old actor John Wilkes Booth, a Southern sympathizer angry with the Confederacy's loss, snuck into the presidential box (bodyguard John F. Parker was away from his post) and shot Lincoln in the back of the head. Lincoln died of the wound at 7:22 A.M. on April 15, 1865.

After escaping the theater, Booth was tracked down on April 26 on a farm near Bowling Green, Virginia. Federal troops set fire to the barn he was hiding in, and he died either by gunshot or due to the fire (stories conflict). Four other people were executed for taking part in Booth's broad assassination plot, which included unsuccessful attempts on the lives of Vice President Andrew Johnson and Secretary of State William Seward.

JAMES ABRAM GARFIELD

After supporting Garfield in the election of 1880, 39-year-old Charles J. Guiteau came to Washington, D.C., expecting a diplomatic appointment. Rebuffed, he decided to kill Garfield, in order to enable Chester Arthur to become President. On July 2, 1881, while the President and Secretary of State James Blaine were waiting at the Baltimore and Potomac railroad station, Guiteau shot Garfield twice. One bullet only grazed Garfield, but the other entered his back and lodged in his abdomen.

Garfield lingered over the summer, seemed to rally for a while, and even had himself taken to Elberon, New Jersey, for the sea air. He died on September 19, of blood poisoning (from unsanitary medical practices) and bronchopneumonia. Guiteau's trial ran from November 1881 to January 1882, after which he was convicted, and hanged on June 30, 1882.

WILLIAM McKINLEY

President William McKinley was in a receiving line at the Pan American Exposition in Buffalo, New York, on September 6, 1901, when 28-year-old anarchist Leon F. Czolgosz shot him twice at point-blank range. The first bullet bounced off a button, but the second entered the President's abdomen, ripping his stomach, kidney, and pancreas. Doctors sewed up the wounds and later performed a minor operation to remove a bit of clothing from the wound, but didn't find the bullet. The President at first appeared to rally, but then developed heart trouble, which digitalis did not cure. McKinley died September 14 at 2:15 A.M., of gangrene around the bullet holes and along the track of the bullet.

Czolgosz refused representation at his trial, saying that, as an anarchist, he didn't recognize the court's authority. Counsel was nevertheless provided, the trial was held (it took nine hours on September 23), he was convicted, and executed by electric chair on October 29.

JOHN FITZGERALD KENNEDY

In perhaps the most studied and most questioned assassination in history, 24-year-old Lee Harvey Oswald shot President John Kennedy in a motorcade on November 22, 1963. Kennedy was in Dallas for public appearances and was traveling in an open limousine with the First Lady, Texas Governor John Connally, and his wife. At 12:30 P.M., three bullets were fired, wounding Connally and hitting Kennedy in the head. Kennedy was rushed to a hospital, and declared dead at 1:00 P.M.

On November 24, while Oswald was being transferred to the

county jail, nightclub owner Jack Ruby shot him to death. Since Oswald wasn't tried, the Warren Commission, appointed by President Lyndon Johnson, determined the facts of the case, and decided that Oswald had been guilty. Later investigations claimed that there had been additional shooters, or other conspiracies. None have been conclusively proved, and will probably always remain a mystery.

26

Presidential Victims of the 20-Year Curse

BEGINNING WITH THE ELECTION OF 1840, EVERY PRESIDENT elected in a year that ended in zero died in office. The curse seemed even more plausible when considering that, of all the Presidents who died in office, only one was not elected in a "zero" year (Zachary Taylor, who was elected in 1848 and died in 1850).

The curse seemed to be in effect again when Ronald Reagan (first elected in 1980) was shot on March 30, 1981. The doctors who treated him said that, after losing so much blood, he might have survived only five more minutes if he hadn't arrived at the hospital and been treated as quickly as he was. Reagan survived emergency surgery and went on to be reelected and serve out his full eight-year term, breaking the curse that had stood for more than a century and a quarter.

The Presidents elected in "zero" years who did not die in office are: Thomas Jefferson (1800), James Monroe (1820), Ronald Reagan (1980), and, at the time of this writing, George W. Bush (2000).

Victims of the 20-Year Curse were:

1. WILLIAM HENRY HARRISON. The ninth President was the oldest man to become President. He was elected in 1840, and on March 4, 1841, delivered a nearly two-hour inaugural address in bad weather without a hat or coat. He developed pneumonia, and died of it one month later, April 4, 1841, in the White House. He died so quickly after taking office that his wife, who had been planning to come to Washington in the spring, never lived in the White House. Harrison was the first President to die in office.

2. ABRAHAM LINCOLN. Elected over Democrat Stephen A. Douglas and National Democrat John C. Breckenridge in the election of 1860, Lincoln's election precipitated the secession of the southern states and the Civil War, which defined his presidency. He was reelected in 1864, with a southerner, Andrew Johnson, as his new Vice President, in an attempt to heal the country. Lincoln's second inaugural was in March 1861, and the Confederacy surrendered on April 9. On the night of April 14, Lincoln was shot in the head by southern sympathizer John Wilkes Booth. He was the first President to be assassinated.

3. JAMES ABRAM GARFIELD won an incredibly close election in 1880 (he won the popular vote, 48.3 to 48.2 percent), and took office in March 1881. On July 2, 1881, Charles J. Guiteau, who had hoped for a diplomatic appointment, shot Garfield while he was waiting at a Washington railroad station. Garfield died from those wounds on September 19.

4. WILLIAM McKINLEY, a Republican, was elected over Democrat William Jennings Bryan in 1896 and again in 1900. After his reelection in 1900, McKinley was shot by anarchist Leon F. Czolgosz on September 6, 1901, in Buffalo, New York, and died of the wound on September 14.

5. WARREN GAMALIEL HARDING won the Republican presidential nomination as a compromise candidate in 1920. In the summer of 1923, Harding took an extended trip to the western United States, to give speeches and meet the people. On that trip, he became the first President to visit Alaska. On July 27 he went to bed in San Francisco, California, complaining of symptoms that were diagnosed as food poisoning. On July 29 he developed pneumonia. He suffered what was assumed to be a stroke in the evening of August 1 (Mrs. Harding did not permit an autopsy), and died on August 2, 1923.

6. FRANKLIN DELANO ROOSEVELT was the only President to serve in a wheelchair (he contracted polio in 1921), and the only President to be elected to a third and a fourth term. First elected in 1932, he was reelected in 1936, 1940, and 1944. On April 12, 1945, he was vacationing in Warm Springs, Georgia, when he apparently suffered a cerebral hemorrhage (brought on by increasing arteriosclerosis and high blood pressure). He died a few hours later, never having regained consciousness.

7. JOHN FITZGERALD KENNEDY. The youngest President elected to the office—Theodore Roosevelt was younger when he succeeded upon William McKinley's death—John Kennedy was elected in 1960. On November 22, 1963, he went to Dallas in an attempt to reconcile opposing factions of the Democratic Party. An hour after landing, while riding in an open limousine in a motorcade through the city, he was shot. One of the bullets passed through his neck and another shattered his skull. He was pronounced dead at 1:00 P.M. (Governor John Connally of Texas, riding with Kennedy, was also wounded.) His assassin, Lee Harvey Oswald, was himself shot to death two days later.

27

Posthumous Presidents
(Those Born After Their Father's Death)

THREE OF THE PRESIDENTS WERE BORN AFTER THEIR FATHERS DIED.

1. ANDREW JACKSON's father, also named Andrew Jackson, injured himself lifting a log, and died the first week of March 1767. President Andrew Jackson, the senior Jackson's third son, was born about two weeks later, on March 15, 1767.

2. RUTHERFORD BIRCHARD HAYES. His father, Rutherford Hayes, contracted a fever and died suddenly on July 20, 1822. About 11 weeks later, on October 4, 1822, Rutherford Hayes's fifth child, the future President, was born.

3. BILL CLINTON. His father, William Jefferson Blythe, Jr., died in a freak automobile accident on May 17, 1946, when his car blew a tire and slipped off the road. He was thrown from the car, hit on the head (knocking him unconscious), and then landed facedown in a puddle, in which he drowned. His son, William Jefferson Blythe 3rd, was born on August 19, 1946. The future President changed his last name to that of his stepfather, Roger Clinton, when he was 16.

TWO

HOME AND FAMILY

The Five Presidents Who Had the Most Children

THE 42 MEN WHO HAVE SERVED AS PRESIDENT WERE A PROLIFIC LOT. Between them, they fathered an acknowledged 156 children— 89 boys and 67 girls (not counting stepchildren or adopted children, although the list does include Warren Harding's illegitimate daughter by Nan Britton)—of whom 121 lived to adulthood. At least 96 presidential children had children of their own, making the 42 Presidents responsible for at least 335 grandchildren. The "average" President would have had 2.1 sons, 1.6 daughters, and eight grandchildren.

1. The most prolific President was JOHN TYLER (1841–45), who fathered 15 children (eight sons and seven daughters), 14 of whom survived to adulthood. Tyler's first wife, Letitia Christian, bore eight children between 1815 and 1830. She died in 1842, two months before her 52nd birthday. Tyler then married Julia Gardiner, who was 30 years younger than he, in June 1844, while he was President. Together, they went on to have seven children between 1846 and 1860. Of the 15 Tyler children, only his sixth, Anna Contesse, died in infancy. The rest survived to adulthood, and between them produced 47 grandchildren. Tyler's last born, Pearl, died in 1947, 157 years after her father had been born.

2. The second-most prolific President, WILLIAM HENRY HARRISON, fathered ten children (six sons and four daughters) between 1796 and 1814, all of them with Anna Tuthill, his only wife. Nine of Harrison's children survived to adulthood, including John Scott Harrison, who was the father of President Benjamin Harrison. The nine Harrison children combined to give their father 43 grandchildren. Harrison was the oldest man elected President when he took office in 1841, and the first to die in office. His Vice President and successor was John Tyler, who is number one on this list.

3. RUTHERFORD B. HAYES (1877–81) and his wife, Lucy Ware Webb Hayes, had eight children (seven sons and one daughter) between 1853 and 1873. Five of them survived to adulthood, giving Hayes nine grandchildren. The last of his children to die was his youngest daughter, Frances "Fanny," who lived 83 years and died in 1950, 57 years after her father.

4. JAMES ABRAM GARFIELD succeeded Hayes, and follows him on this list, having had seven children (five sons and two daughters) between 1860 and 1874 with his wife, Lucretia Rudolph. Five of them survived to adulthood, giving Garfield 14 grandchildren. One of his sons, James Rudolph, served as Theodore Roosevelt's Secretary of the Interior from 1907 to 1909. His longest-lived son, Abram, lived 86 years and died in 1958, 77 years after his father.

5. Five Presidents are tied for fifth place on this list, siring six children each. They are: THOMAS JEFFERSON (1801–09), ZACHARY TAYLOR (1849–50), THEODORE ROOSEVELT (1901–09), FRANKLIN DELANO ROOSEVELT (1933–45), and GEORGE H.W. BUSH (1989–93).

★ THOMAS JEFFERSON's five daughters and one son don't include his children by his slave, Sally Hemmings. He didn't officially recognize them as his children during his life, but later evidence makes it a near certainty that some or all of Hemmings's children were Jefferson's.

★ ZACHARY TAYLOR had five daughters and one son. The longest-lived was fifth daughter Mary Elizabeth, who died in 1909, aged 85.

★ THEODORE ROOSEVELT's first daughter, Alice Lee, was the child of his first wife, Alice Hathaway Lee. She was also his longest-lived child, dying in 1980 at the age of 96. His other daughter, Ethel Carow, and all four sons, were the children of his second wife, Edith Kermit Carow.

★ Two of FRANKLIN DELANO ROOSEVELT's five sons, James and Franklin Delano, Jr., served in the House of Representatives. Franklin Delano, Jr., also served as Under Secretary of Commerce from 1962 to 1965.

★ GEORGE H.W. BUSH had four sons and two daughters. His oldest child, George W. Bush, was elected President in 2000. One of his daughters, Robin, died of leukemia at age four.

29

The Presidents Who Had the Fewest Children

THOUGH MANY PRESIDENTS WERE QUITE PROLIFIC, FIVE OF THEM had no children at all, and a further three fathered one each.

Neither James Knox Polk (1845–49) nor James Buchanan (1857–61) had any children. Polk was married to Sarah Childress from the age of 28 until his death 25 years later (she outlived him by 42 years). Buchanan was the only President to never marry.

Neither George Washington (1789–97) nor James Madison (1809–17) had any children, but both married widows and were stepfather to their wives' children. In 1759, Washington married 27-year-old widow Martha Dandridge Custis, who was about eight months older than him. At the time, her two younger children, John "Jack" Parke and Martha "Patsy" Parke, were five and four (her two older children each died at the age of four). In 1794, 43-year-old Madison married 26-year-old widow Dolley Payne Todd, and took in her two-year-old son, John Payne Todd.

Andrew Jackson (1829–37) and his wife, Rachel Donelson, had no children. In 1810, when they were both 42, they adopted her brother's one-month-old son, and named him Andrew Jackson, Jr.

Three Presidents had one child each: Warren Harding (1921–23), Harry Truman (1945–53), and Bill Clinton (1993–2001).

★ HARDING's illegitimate daughter, Elizabeth Ann Christian, daughter of his mistress, Nan Britton, was born in 1919, when he was 54. She died in 2005.

★ TRUMAN's daughter, Mary Margaret (known as Margaret), born in 1924, was a well-known mystery writer. She died in 2008.

★ CLINTON's daughter, Chelsea, was born in 1980.

30

Ten Presidents Who Were the Most Older Than Their Wives

SOME PRESIDENTS WERE MUCH OLDER THAN THEIR WIVES, EITHER because they married late in life or found very young brides. The average President's first (or only) wife was four years, 108 days younger than he was. Counting all wives, both first marriages and seconds, the average President was five years, 316 days older than his wife. Those Presidents who were the most older than their first wives include:

1. GROVER CLEVELAND (1885–89 and 1893–97), born March 18, 1837, was 27 years, 125 days older than his wife, Frances Folsom (born July 21, 1864). Frances was his law partner's daughter, and became his ward when she was 11. They married in 1886, after he'd been President a little more than one year, making him the only President to get married in the White House. After his death in 1908, she remarried, becoming the first presidential widow to remarry. She died in 1947.

2. JAMES MADISON (1809–17) was born March 16, 1751. In 1794 he married Dolley Payne Todd, a 26-year-old widow who was 17 years, 65 days younger than him (she was born May 20, 1768). She served as Thomas Jefferson's official hostess while her hus-

band was Secretary of State, and outlived him by 13 years, dying in 1849.

3. JOHN FITZGERALD KENNEDY (1961–63) was the youngest President elected (he'd been born May 29, 1917). In 1953 he married Jacqueline Lee Bouvier, who was 12 years, 60 days younger than him (she'd been born July 28, 1929). After his assassination in 1963, she married Greek shipping tycoon Aristotle Onassis in 1968 (he died in 1975). She died in 1994 and was buried next to Kennedy in Arlington National Cemetery.

4. JAMES MONROE (1817–25) was ten years, 63 days older than his wife, Elizabeth Kortright. He was born April 28, 1758, she on June 30, 1768. They married in 1786, while she was still 17. In 1820, their daughter Maria married her first cousin in the first White House wedding. President Monroe died in 1831, less than a year after his wife.

5. ABRAHAM LINCOLN (1861–65) was nine years, 315 days older than his wife, Mary Todd. He was born on February 12, 1809, she on December 13, 1818. They were married in late 1842, and after suffering the deaths of one son in 1862, her husband in 1865 (by assassination), and another son in 1871, she died in 1882.

Six Presidents remarried (five after the deaths of their wives, one after divorce). In five of these cases, their second wives were much younger (for more details on these marriages, see Chapter 34: "The Six Presidents Who Had More Than One Wife"). The average President who married twice was 16 years, 217 days older than his second wife. The greatest age gaps were:

1. JOHN TYLER (1841–45) was 30 years, 36 days older than Julia Gardiner, his second wife, who was the first woman to marry a sitting President.

2. BENJAMIN HARRISON (1889–93) was 24 years, 253 days older than Mary Scott Lord Dimmick, his first wife's niece, whom he married after retiring from the presidency.

3. WOODROW WILSON (1913–21). His second wife, Edith Bolling Galt, was 15 years, 291 days younger than him. She outlived him by 37 years, dying on December 28, 1961, which would have been Wilson's 105th birthday.

4. MILLARD FILLMORE (1850–53). His first wife, Abigail Powers, caught a cold at the inauguration of Fillmore's successor, Franklin Pierce, and died a few weeks later. Five years later he married 44-year-old widow Caroline Carmichael McIntosh, who was 13 years, 287 days younger than him.

5. RONALD REAGAN (1981–89) divorced his first wife, Jane Wyman, in 1948, after eight years of marriage. He then married Nancy Davis, 12 years, 150 days his junior, on March 4, 1952. They remained married until his death in 2004.

31

The Six Presidents Younger Than Their Wives

ONLY SIX OF THE 41 PRESIDENTS WHO MARRIED CHOSE WIVES WHO were older than they were.

1. WARREN HARDING (1921–23). On July 8, 1891, 25-year-old Harding married 30-year-old divorcée Florence Mabel Kling DeWolfe. She was born on August 15, 1860, five years, 79 days

before he was. Following his death in office in 1923, she retired to her Ohio home, and died 16 months later.

2. MILLARD FILLMORE (1850–53). In early 1826 he married Abigail Powers, who was one year, 296 days older (she was born on March 17, 1798, he on January 7, 1800). She had two children, and as First Lady, pushed Congress into funding the White House's first permanent library. She died less than a month after her husband left office, having caught a cold at his successor's inaugural. Fillmore remarried five years later.

3. BENJAMIN HARRISON (1889–93). In late 1853 he married Caroline Lavinia Scott. He was 20 (born August 20, 1833), she 21 (born October 1, 1832). She was the first president-general of the Daughters of the American Revolution, and had two children with Harrison. She contracted tuberculosis during her husband's reelection campaign, and died two weeks before he lost that election. Harrison married his deceased wife's niece four years later.

4. RICHARD NIXON (1969–74). Nixon married Thelma Catherine "Pat" Ryan in 1940. She was 299 days older than he, having been born March 16, 1912. They remained married through his resignation from the presidency, until her death in 1993. He died 304 days later, on April 22, 1994.

5. GEORGE WASHINGTON (1789–97). In January 1759, Washington married 27-year-old widow Martha Dandridge Custis, who had two young children. Having been born June 21, 1731, she was 246 days older than him. She was the only First Lady to live in New York, and the first of two to live in Philadelphia (before the capital was moved to Washington, DC, in 1800). She outlived her husband, who died at the end of 1799, by two and a half years.

6. HERBERT HOOVER (1929–33). Hoover and Lou Henry met in college, and waited to complete their educations before getting

married on February 10, 1899. She was 134 days older than he was (she was born on March 20, 1874, he on August 10 of the same year), and followed him on assignments around the world, including in China during the Boxer Rebellion. After their one term in the White House, they moved to New York City, where Lou died of a heart attack in 1944. Her husband, the longest-retired President, died 20 years later.

32

The Five Presidents Whose Wives Outlived Them the Longest

SOME PRESIDENTS DIED LONG BEFORE THEIR WIVES, BUT NOT ALL of them died in office. Of the 35 sets of Presidents and first wives who are both deceased, 20 wives outlived their husbands. On average, the wives outlived their husbands by two years, 309 days. As for the Presidents who married more than once—in all five cases, the wife outlived the husband. Factoring them in, the average that all these wives outlived their President husbands becomes six years, 82 days.

1. JAMES KNOX POLK (1845–49) died three months after leaving office, on June 15, 1849. His wife, Sarah Childress, outlived him by 42 years, 60 days, dying on August 14, 1891.

2. GROVER CLEVELAND (1885–89, 1893–97), married his 21-year-old ward Frances Folsom during his first term of office. They

were married for 22 years before he died on June 24, 1908. She remarried in 1913 and died October 29, 1947, 39 years, 127 days after her President husband.

3. JAMES ABRAM GARFIELD (1881) was shot a few months into his first year in office, and died on September 19, 1881, before his 50th birthday. His wife, Lucretia, survived him by 36 years, 166 days, dying on March 4, 1918, less than a month before her 86th birthday.

4. LYNDON BAINES JOHNSON (1963–69) died four years after retiring from the presidency, on January 22, 1973, before his 65th birthday. His widow, Claudia Alta "Lady Bird" Taylor, died at the age of 94, on July 11, 2007. She survived her husband by 34 years, 170 days.

5. JOHN FITZGERALD KENNEDY (1961–63) was the youngest President to be elected, and his wife, Jacqueline Lee Bouvier, was 12 years younger than he was. He was assassinated in 1963, and she married Aristotle Onassis five years later (he died in 1975). She died 30 years, 178 days after her President husband, on May 19, 1994, and was buried beside him in Arlington National Cemetery.

Gerald Ford died on December 26, 2006. He and his wife, Elizabeth "Betty" Bloomer, will move into the fifth position on this list on June 22, 2036, if she lives to be 118 years old.

Second Wives Who Outlived Their President Husbands

The five deceased second wives have outlived their presidential husbands by an average of 29 years, 318 days. The longest times are:

1. BENJAMIN HARRISON (1889–93) married his second wife, Mary Scott Lord Dimmick, three years after leaving office, in 1896. He

died on March 13, 1901. The second Mrs. Harrison, who was the first Mrs. Harrison's niece, outlived her husband by 46 years, 298 days, dying on January 5, 1948.

2. WOODROW WILSON (1913–21) was widowed in the White House. His first wife, Ellen Louise Axson, died on August 6, 1914. Soon afterward he met Edith Bolling Galt, who was a widow. They married in late 1915, and she nursed him through his stroke in 1919. After leaving the White House, he died on February 3, 1924. The second Mrs. Wilson outlived him by 37 years, 328 days, dying on December 28, 1961.

3. THEODORE ROOSEVELT (1901–09) lost his first wife after less than three years of marriage, in 1884. He married Edith Kermit Carow in 1886, and together they had five more children. He retired from the presidency in 1909, then attempted to come back in the election of 1912 but lost to Wilson. He died on January 6, 1919. Edith, less than three years younger than her husband, outlived him by 29 years, 268 days, dying on September 30, 1948.

4. JOHN TYLER (1841–45) became a widower while serving as President, as his first wife, Letitia Christian, died on September 10, 1842. On June 26, 1844, he married Julia Gardiner, who was 30 years younger (and younger than his three oldest children). After leaving the White House, retired President Tyler and his second wife had seven children. The last, Pearl, was born in 1860, when Tyler was 70 years old. He died before Pearl's second birthday, on January 18, 1862. Julia outlived him by 27 years, 173 days, dying on July 10, 1889.

5. MILLARD FILLMORE (1850–53) lost his first wife, Abigail Powers, 26 days after leaving office. Five years later he married 44-year-old widow Caroline Carmichael McIntosh, and they had 16 years together. After his death on March 8, 1874, she survived another seven years, 156 days, dying on August 11, 1881.

Ronald Reagan died on June 5, 2004. He and his wife, Nancy Davis, will move into the fifth position on this list on November 9, 2011, when she is 88 years old.

33

The Five Presidents Who Outlived Their Wives the Longest

ONLY 15 OF THE PRESIDENTS OUTLIVED THEIR WIVES (NOT COUNT-ing those Presidents and presidential wives who are still alive). On average, the 39 presidential wives outlived their husbands by five years, 183 days. However, of those Presidents who did outlive their wives, some did so by many years. The five who lived the longest without their wives:

1. THOMAS JEFFERSON (1801–09) and 23-year-old widow Martha Wayles Skelton were married on January 1, 1772. They had six children—two of whom lived to adulthood—before she died on September 6, 1782. Jefferson never remarried, and outlived his wife by 43 years, 304 days, dying on July 4, 1826. Dolley Madison, wife of his Secretary of State James Madison—who would succeed him as President—served as his official White House hostess.

2. MARTIN VAN BUREN (1837–41) married Hannah Hoes, his first cousin once removed, on February 21, 1807. They had five children—four of whom lived to adulthood—before she died on February 5, 1819. Van Buren never remarried, and outlived his wife by 43 years, 169 days, dying on July 24, 1862.

3. THEODORE ROOSEVELT (1901–09) married Alice Hathaway Lee when he was 21 and she was 19, on October 27, 1880. Together they had a daughter, Alice Lee, but his wife died two days after the child's birth, on February 14, 1884. In December 1886 he married Edith Kermit Carow, who was eight days younger than his first wife and would outlive him by nearly 30 years. But between the death of his first wife and his own death, on January 6, 1919, 34 years and 326 days passed.

4. MILLARD FILLMORE (1850–53) married Abigail Powers, who was nearly two years older, on February 5, 1826. They had two children. Upon Fillmore's retirement, they attended the inauguration of his successor, Franklin Pierce, when Abigail caught a cold. She died on March 30, 1853, 26 days after moving out of the White House. Fillmore remarried five years later. He died on March 8, 1874, having outlived his first wife by 20 years, 343 days.

5. HERBERT HOOVER (1929–33) married Lou Henry on February 10, 1899. They had two children, and were together until her death on January 7, 1944. Hoover was the longest-retired President, surviving the office by more than 31 years, and outliving his wife by 20 years, 287 days. He died on October 20, 1964.

34

The Six Presidents Who Had More Than One Wife

OF THE 42 PRESIDENTS, 35 HAD ONE WIFE, ONE (JAMES BUCHANAN) never married, and six had two wives (not counting Andrew Jackson, who married his one wife twice). The six included five widowers and one divorcé.

1. JOHN TYLER (1841–45) married his first wife, Letitia Christian, on his 23rd birthday, March 29, 1813. They had eight children over the next 17 years, and then moved into the White House when William Henry Harrison died in April 1841, making Tyler the President. Letitia died on September 10, 1842. Soon afterward he met Julia Gardiner, who was 30 years younger (and younger than his three oldest children). They married on June 26, 1844, in New York City (making Tyler the first President to marry while in office), and had seven children together over the next 16 years. Tyler died in 1862; Julia outlived him by 27 years, dying in 1889.

2. MILLARD FILLMORE (1850–53) married Abigail Powers in 1826. Together, they had two children. They moved into the White House when Zachary Taylor's death elevated Fillmore to the presidency. Fillmore wasn't nominated for his own term in 1852, and retired on March 4, 1853. Abigail caught a cold at the inau-

gural ceremonies for Franklin Pierce, Fillmore's successor, and died 26 days later. Five years after that, Fillmore married Caroline Carmichael McIntosh, a widow 13 years his junior. They had 16 years together before Fillmore died in 1874; Caroline outlived him by seven years.

3. BENJAMIN HARRISON (1889–93) married Caroline Lavinia Scott when he was 20, in 1853. They had three children, two of whom survived to adulthood, and were together when he won the presidential election of 1888. On October 25, 1892, two weeks before he lost his bid for reelection, Caroline died in the White House. In 1896, Harrison married 37-year-old widow Mary Scott Lord Dimmick, who was his first wife's niece. Harrison and Mary had a daughter in 1897. Harrison died in 1901; Mary in 1948.

4. THEODORE ROOSEVELT (1901–09) married Alice Hathaway Lee in 1880. She died on February 14, 1884, two days after giving birth to her only daughter, Alice Lee. He was devastated by her death and that of his mother (who died the same day in the same house), and traveled to the West for two and a half years. Soon after his return to New York, he married Edith Kermit Carow on December 2, 1886. They had five children in the next eleven years, and were together until his death in 1919. Edith lived another 29 years, dying in 1948.

5. WOODROW WILSON (1913–21) married Ellen Louise Axson in 1885, when he was 28. They had three children in three years, and moved to Washington when he won the election of 1912. Ellen died of Bright's disease on August 6, 1914. The following March, Wilson was introduced to Edith Bolling Galt, a widow 15 years his junior. They married on December 18, 1915, at her home in Washington, D.C. Following Wilson's stroke in September 1919, Edith—nearly the only person who saw him—was

probably acting as President in his stead for about six months. After his recovery, they retired in 1921. Wilson lived just three years as a retired President, dying in 1924. Edith outlived him by 37 years, attending John Kennedy's inauguration, and dying on December 28, 1961, at the age of 89.

6. RONALD REAGAN (1981–89) is the only President to have been divorced. As an actor in Hollywood, he married actress Sarah Jane Faulks, known as Jane Wyman, in 1940, two weeks before his 29th birthday (she was three years younger). Together, they had a daughter, adopted a son, and then had another daughter, who died the day after her birth in 1947. They divorced in 1948. In 1952, Reagan married another actress, Anne Frances Robbins, who went by the name Nancy Davis, and who was 12 years younger than him. They had a daughter and a son. Reagan tried for the Republican nomination in 1976, but lost out to sitting President Ford. He was nominated in 1980, and became the oldest person to be elected and to serve as President. After leaving office in 1989, he made few public appearances, and several years later, announced he had Alzheimer's disease. He was rarely seen after that, and died in 2004.

35

The President Who Had No Wife

OF THE 42 MEN TO SERVE AS PRESIDENT, ONLY ONE WAS A LIFELONG bachelor. James Buchanan (1857–61) did get engaged in the summer of 1819, when he was 28. Anne Coleman, his intended, was 23, and after an argument, broke off the engagement. She went to visit relatives, and died suddenly on December 9, 1819, possibly of suicide. Buchanan's niece, Harriet Lane, served as official White House hostess during his administration, but there is no evidence of any other romance in his life. Buchanan died in 1868.

The Four Presidents Who Had No Wife While in Office

Four Presidents were married at one time, but were alone during their years in the White House:

1. THOMAS JEFFERSON (1801–09) married Martha Wayles Skelton on January 1, 1772. She died on September 6, 1782, two months before her 34th birthday. Jefferson never remarried, although he is assumed to have had a long affair with his slave, Sally Hemmings. He died in 1826.

2. ANDREW JACKSON (1829–37) married Rachel Donelson Robards on January 17, 1794. She died on December 22, 1828—three weeks after the presidential electors had cast their ballots to elect Jackson the seventh President—at the age of 61. Jackson served his two terms as a widower President, and died in 1845.

3. MARTIN VAN BUREN (1837–41) married Hannah Hoes on February 21, 1807. They had five children in the next ten years. She died on February 5, 1819, a month before her 36th birthday. Van Buren never remarried, and died in 1862.

4. CHESTER ALAN ARTHUR (1881–85) married Ellen Lewis Herndon on October 25, 1859. She died on January 12, 1880, at the age of 42. Arthur didn't remarry, but his sister, Mary Arthur McElroy, served as his White House hostess. He died in November 1886, less than two years after leaving office.

36

The Three Presidents Who Got Married While in Office

MARRIAGE IS USUALLY CONSIDERED AN EARLIER-IN-LIFE EVENT THAN running for President, and in modern times, the nearly 24-hour-a-day schedule of the presidency leaves little time for things like dating. But three of our Presidents did manage to get married while in office. Two of them were widowers who remarried, while the other married for the first time.

1. JOHN TYLER (1841–45) married Letitia Christian on March 29, 1813. They had eight children together. On April 4, 1841, President William Henry Harrison died after one month in office, elevating Vice President Tyler to the presidency. On September 10, 1842, Letitia died, leaving Tyler a widower in office. But he wasn't alone for long. On June 26, 1844, he married Julia Gardiner, becoming the first President to marry in office.

2. GROVER CLEVELAND (1885–89 and 1893–97) was the second bachelor elected President (after James Buchanan). Unlike Buchanan, however, he managed to get married while he was President. On June 2, 1886, the 49-year-old President married 21-year-old Frances Folsom in the White House. Of the five Cleveland children, the first, Ruth, was born between his two

terms as President. Esther was born in the White House in September 1893, Marion was born in Massachusetts in July 1895, and Richard and Francis were both born after Cleveland retired from the presidency.

3. WOODROW WILSON (1913–21) married Ellen Louise Axson on June 24, 1885. She was 25, he 30. They had three children, all of whom saw their father elected President. Ellen died in the White House on August 6, 1914, but Wilson wasn't alone for long. He was soon introduced to Edith Bolling Galt, a widow 16 years his junior. He courted her, and married her on December 18, 1915, in her home in Washington, D.C. Wilson died in 1924, having been in poor health since his stroke in 1919.

37

Most Popular Religions of Presidents

ALL 42 PRESIDENTS HAVE PROFESSED BELIEF IN SOME FORM OF Christianity, though some were more religious than others. And the amount of religious fervor shown by the Presidents seems to vary over time, as with the general populace. Of the Christian denominations, the most popular with Presidents are:

1. EPISCOPALIAN. Ten of the Presidents were Episcopalian, and three others were Episcopalians at some time in their lives: GEORGE WASHINGTON, JAMES MADISON, JAMES MONROE, WILLIAM HENRY HARRISON, ZACHARY TAYLOR, FRANKLIN PIERCE, CHESTER ALAN ARTHUR, FRANKLIN DELANO ROOSEVELT, GERALD FORD,

and GEORGE H.W. BUSH. JOHN TYLER was an Episcopalian in general, but in practice more of a deist. RUTHERFORD HAYES was Presbyterian by birth, Episcopalian as a single adult, and then a Methodist (his wife's religion) after marriage. GEORGE W. BUSH was born Episcopalian, became Methodist after marrying Laura, and then became a born-again Christian.

2. PRESBYTERIAN. Seven of the Presidents were lifelong Presbyterians, and another three were Presbyterian at some time in their lives. The seven are: ANDREW JACKSON, JAMES BUCHANAN, ABRAHAM LINCOLN, GROVER CLEVELAND, BENJAMIN HARRISON, WOODROW WILSON, and DWIGHT EISENHOWER. JAMES KNOX POLK and RUTHERFORD HAYES were both Presbyterian by birth, but later became Methodists. RONALD REAGAN was a Disciple of Christ, but sometimes identified himself as a Presbyterian.

3. METHODIST. Two Presidents were lifelong Methodists: ULYSSES GRANT and WILLIAM MCKINLEY. Another three became Methodists after their marriages: JAMES KNOX POLK, RUTHERFORD HAYES, and GEORGE W. BUSH.

4 (tie). UNITARIAN. Four Presidents were Unitarians: JOHN ADAMS, JOHN QUINCY ADAMS, MILLARD FILLMORE, and WILLIAM HOWARD TAFT.

4 (tie). BAPTIST. Four Presidents were Baptists: WARREN G. HARDING, HARRY S TRUMAN, JIMMY CARTER, and BILL CLINTON.

Other presidential religions, practiced at some point during their lives, include: Anglican, Dutch Reformed, Disciples of Christ, Congregationalist, Quaker, and Roman Catholic.

38

Presidents with Foreign-Born Wives

THE ONLY TRULY FOREIGN-BORN PRESIDENTIAL WIFE WAS LOUISA Johnson, the wife of John Quincy Adams. She was born on February 12, 1775, in London, England. Her father, Joshua Johnson of Baltimore, Maryland, was in London serving as the American consul-general. So, though she was born in England, her parents were American.

Other than Mrs. Adams, every presidential wife born on American soil before the Declaration of Independence was, theoretically, a foreign-born wife. They were born subjects of Great Britain. Those British presidential wives (whose President-husbands were also born British) were:

MARTHA DANDRIDGE CUSTIS WASHINGTON, born June 21, 1731, in New Kent County, Virginia

ABIGAIL SMITH ADAMS, born November 22, 1744, in Weymouth, Massachusetts

MARTHA WAYLES SKELTON JEFFERSON, born October 30, 1748, in Charles City County, Virginia

DOLLEY PAYNE TODD MADISON, born May 20, 1768, in Guilford County, North Carolina

ELIZABETH KORTRIGHT MONROE, born June 30, 1768, in Oak Hill, Loudoun County, Virginia

RACHEL DONELSON ROBARDS JACKSON, born June 15, 1767, in Pittsylvania County, Virginia

ANNA TUTHILL SYMMES HARRISON, born July 25, 1775, in Flatbrook, Sussex County, New Jersey

39

Presidents Whose Parents Lived to See Them Inaugurated

A REMARKABLE NUMBER OF PRESIDENTIAL PARENTS HAVE SEEN their sons become President: seven fathers and 14 mothers. Sadly, nearly half of them (three fathers and seven mothers) died during their son's term of office. Twenty-four Presidents had no parents alive at the time of their inauguration.

George Washington's mother, Mary Ball Washington, was born about 1709 and died in 1789, during her son's first year as the first President. Their relationship was said to be always strained and distant.

John Adams's mother, Susanna Boylston Adams, was born in 1709 and died in 1797, during her son's first year as President. Her husband, the President's father, died in 1761, and in 1766—more than a year after John married—she married a man named John Hall, who didn't get along with her grown children.

James Madison's mother, Eleanor "Nelly" Rose Conway Madison, born in 1731, was 78 when her son became President, and died in 1829 at the age of 98. She and her President-son had a close relationship.

John Quincy Adams's father, the second President, was the first man to live to see his son inaugurated as President. Born in 1735, he was 89 when his son was inaugurated. He died on July 4, 1826, during John Quincy's second year in office.

James Knox Polk's mother, Jane Knox Polk, was born in 1776. She lived to see her son inaugurated, retired, and buried. Polk was the first President who did not outlive his mother (she died in 1852, having outlived seven of her ten children).

Millard Fillmore's father, Nathaniel Fillmore, was born in 1771. He lived to see his son inaugurated, and was the first father of a President to visit his son in the White House. He died in 1863, aged 92, having been a widower for 32 years.

Ulysses S. Grant's father, Jesse Root Grant, was born in 1794; his mother, Hannah Simpson Grant, was born in 1798. Grant was the first President whose parents both lived to see him inaugurated. Neither parent attended his inauguration, but Grant's father visited him frequently in the White House. He died in 1873, during Grant's second term. His mother died in 1883, six years after her President-son retired from office and two years before he died.

James Abram Garfield's mother, Eliza Ballou Garfield, was born in 1801. In 1881 she became the first mother of a President to attend his inauguration, and lived in the White House during his term.

William McKinley's mother, Nancy Allison McKinley, was born in 1809. She attended her son's inauguration in 1897, and died later that year.

Warren G. Harding's father, George Tryon Harding, was born in 1843. He saw his son inaugurated, and survived him by five years, dying in 1928. Harding was the first President who did not outlive his father.

Calvin Coolidge's father, John Calvin Coolidge, was born in 1845. He not only lived to see his son take the oath of office, but as a justice of the peace, administered the oath himself (the only President's father to do so). The then–Vice President was visiting his father when President Harding died. The senior Coolidge died in 1926, during his son's term.

Franklin Delano Roosevelt's mother, Sara "Sallie" Delano Roosevelt, was born in 1854. Her husband was 26 years older than she (Sara was his second wife), and died in 1900. Mrs. Roosevelt lived to see her son inaugurated three times, dying in 1941.

Harry S Truman's mother, Martha Ellen Young Truman, was born in 1852 in Missouri. She grew up in a pro-Confederate household, and when she visited her son during his presidency (80 years after the Civil War had ended), she refused to sleep in Abraham Lincoln's bed. She died in 1947, aged 94.

John Fitzgerald Kennedy's father, Joseph Patrick Kennedy, was born in 1888; his mother, Rose Fitzgerald Kennedy, was born in 1890. They were only the second couple to see their son inaugurated.

Jimmy Carter's mother, Lillian Gordy Carter, was born in 1898. She was a registered nurse and Peace Corps volunteer. She attended her son's inauguration in January 1977, and then represented the United States in February 1977 at the funeral of Indian President Fakhruddin Ali Ahmed, revisiting the country in which she'd served in the Peace Corps only a decade earlier. She died of cancer in 1983.

George H.W. Bush's mother, Dorothy Walker Bush, was born in 1901. She was the second woman to be both mother and grandmother to U.S. Presidents. She died in late 1992, two weeks after her son was defeated in his bid for reelection.

Bill Clinton's mother, Virginia Cassidy Blythe Clinton Dwire Kelley, was born about 1923. She was the most-married presidential parent. Her first husband, William Jefferson Blythe, the President's father, died in a car crash in 1946, three years after their marriage (and weeks before the President was born). She divorced her second husband, Roger Clinton (the father of the President's half brother), in 1962, after 12 years of marriage. She remarried him three months later, and then he died in 1967. Then she married Jeff Dwire, who died from diabetes in 1974. Finally, she married Richard Kelley in 1982. She saw her son's inauguration, but died a year later, in January 1994.

George W. Bush's parents, President George H.W. Bush (born 1924) and Barbara Pierce Bush (born 1925), are only the third set of presidential parents to both see their son inaugurated President (after Grant and Kennedy).

40

Presidents Known for Having Facial Hair

MANY MEN HAVE TRIED FACIAL HAIR AT SOME POINT IN THEIR lives; some have found they preferred the look, others did not. The following Presidents' best-known images include facial hair of some type.

Abraham Lincoln (1861–65) is the only President to have worn a beard with no mustache.

Ulysses S. Grant (1869–77), Rutherford B. Hayes (1877–81), James A. Garfield (1881), and Benjamin Harrison (1889–93) all had a full beard and mustache.

Chester A. Arthur (1881–85), Grover Cleveland (1885–89, 1893–97), Theodore Roosevelt (1901–09), and William H. Taft (1909–13) all had mustaches but no beards.

Were Presidents fashion trendsetters, or merely trend followers when it came to their facial hair? All of the mustache/beard combinations appeared during one quarter of a century, and all of those with facial hair of any sort were in office during a 52-year span.

41

The President Whose Birthday Was His Wife's Death Day

WOODROW WILSON (1913–21) AND HIS SECOND WIFE, EDITH BOLLING Galt, are the only presidential couple to share dates for these major life events. He was born on December 28, 1856. She died on what would have been his 105th birthday, December 28, 1961.

42

The Seven Presidents Who Changed Their Names

NOT EVERY PRESIDENT WAS BORN WITH THE NAME HE USED throughout life. For a variety of reasons, seven of them changed their names between birth and fame.

1. ULYSSES SIMPSON GRANT (served 1869–77) was born Hiram Ulysses Grant in 1822. As a cadet at West Point, to avoid the unfortunate initials HUG stamped large on his belongings, he began signing his name Ulysses H. Grant. But he later learned that Representative Thomas L. Hamer, who arranged his appointment to West Point, had mistakenly listed him as Ulysses Simpson Grant. At the academy, he was commonly known as U.S. or Uncle Sam, and he adopted the name Representative Hamer gave him.

2. GROVER CLEVELAND (1885–89, 1893–97) was born Stephen Grover Cleveland in 1837. In his late teens he started signing his name S. Grover Cleveland, and a few years later dropped the initial, and the first name, completely.

3. WOODROW WILSON (1913–21) was born Thomas Woodrow Wilson in 1856. After graduating from Princeton, he went by T. Woodrow Wilson, and soon dropped the initial and the name Thomas.

4. CALVIN COOLIDGE (1923–29) was born John Calvin Coolidge in 1872. Named for his father, he was always called Calvin or Cal to avoid confusion at home. He dropped his mostly unused first name after graduating from college.

5. DWIGHT DAVID EISENHOWER (1953–61) was born David Dwight Eisenhower in 1890. Named for his father, he was called by his middle name to avoid confusion at home. By the time he entered West Point, he was signing his name Dwight David Eisenhower, and the reversal of names stuck.

6. GERALD RUDOLPH FORD, JR. (1974–77), was born Leslie Lynch King, Jr., named for his father. His mother divorced his father soon after his birth, and married Gerald Rudolf Ford when the fu-

ture President was about two. Her new husband adopted her son, and they changed his name to Gerald Rudolph Ford, Jr. (with no real explanation for the changed spelling of the middle name).

7. BILL CLINTON (1993–2001) was born William Jefferson Blythe 3rd, named for his father, who died three months before he was born. At age 16 he legally changed his name to that of his stepfather, Roger Clinton, becoming William Jefferson Clinton.

And not so much a changed name as a confusing one: Harry S Truman (1945–53) was named for his maternal uncle, Harrison Young, when he was born in 1884. His parents couldn't decide whether to make his middle name Shippe (for his paternal grandfather, Anderson Shippe Truman) or Solomon (for his maternal grandfather, Solomon Young). In the end, they simply gave him the middle initial S to represent both names. So there is no period following his middle initial, since it doesn't stand for anything.

43

Presidential Relatives Who Served in the Federal Government

GOVERNMENTAL SERVICE HAS, FOR MOST OF THE COUNTRY'S HIStory, been a strictly male occupation, as this list reflects. By far, the presidential relatives who served in government were nearly all males—sons, grandsons, great-grandsons, fathers, brothers, nephews—in fact, all but one sister and one wife.

JOHN ADAMS. His second child (who was his first son), John Quincy Adams, was the sixth President of the United States (1825–29).

His first child, daughter Abigail Adams (1765–1813), married Col. William Stephens Smith (1755–1816) in 1786. He represented New York in the U.S. House of Representatives (1813–15).

The grandson of his brother (Captain Elihu Adams) was Aaron Hobart (1787–1858), who served in Congress.

THOMAS JEFFERSON. His younger daughter, Mary "Maria" (1778–1804), married her half first cousin John Wayles Eppes (1773–1823), who served as a representative and senator (his mother, Elizabeth Wayles, was Maria's mother's half sister).

His grandson—daughter Martha's tenth child—Meriwether Lewis Randolph (1810–37), was Secretary of the Territory of Arkansas (1835–36).

JAMES MADISON. His grandniece, Ann Maury Baldwin (born in 1817, she was the granddaughter of his sister, Nelly Conway Madison), married Isaac Hite Hay, who was the United States consul at Jaffa.

His great-nephew—Ann's son—John Baldwin Hay (born in 1845), was U.S. Consul-General in Constantinople.

JAMES MONROE. His daughter, Eliza Kortright Monroe (1787–1840), married Judge George Hay, who was the U.S. District Attorney who prosecuted Vice President Aaron Burr for treason (1806–07).

His great-great-granddaughter—Eliza's great-granddaughter—Hortense Hay Hardesty (1865–1933), married William Watson McIntire (1850–1912), who served as a member of the House of Representatives.

His grandson—daughter Maria's third child—Samuel Laurence Gouverneur, Jr. (1826–80), was the first U.S. consul at Foo Chow, China, under President Buchanan.

His nephew—brother Andrew's son—Col. James Monroe (1799–1870), was a member of the House of Representatives.

JOHN QUINCY ADAMS. His father, John Adams, was the second President of the United States (1797–1801, see above).

His wife, Louisa Catherine Johnson (1775–1852), was the second daughter of Joshua Johnson of Baltimore, Maryland, who was U.S. Consul-General in London (1785–99).

His son, Charles Francis Adams (1807–86), was a member of Congress, and the U.S. minister to England (1861–68).

His great-grandson—Charles's grandson—Charles Francis Adams III (1866–1954), was U.S. Secretary of the Navy (1929–33).

MARTIN VAN BUREN. His half brother (the son of his mother's first husband), Jacobus Van Alen, was a member of the U.S. House of Representatives (1807–09).

WILLIAM HENRY HARRISON. His father, Benjamin Harrison (1726–91), was a member of the Continental Congress (1774–78) representing Virginia, and signed the Declaration of Independence.

His fifth child, John Scott Harrison (1804–78), was a member of the U.S. House of Representatives (1853–57).

His grandson—John's son—Benjamin Harrison, was President of the United States (1885–89). (For William Henry Harrison's relatives through Benjamin Harrison, see below.)

His brother, Carter Bassett Harrison, was a member of Congress (1793–99).

JOHN TYLER. His second wife, Julia Gardiner (1820–89), was the daughter of U.S. Senator David Gardiner.

His son, Robert Tyler (1816–77), served as his private secretary while he was President, and was later Registrar of the Treasury of the Confederate States of America.

His son, John Tyler (1819–96), was Assistant Secretary of War of the CSA.

His son, (David) Gardiner "Gardie" Tyler (1846–1927), was a member of the U.S. House of Representatives (1893–97).

JAMES KNOX POLK. His brother, William Hawkins Polk (born in 1815), was a member of the U.S. House of Representatives and was U.S. Chargé d'Affaires in the Kingdom of the Two Sicilies.

JAMES BUCHANAN. His grandnephew—his sister Harriet's grandson—Frank Anderson Henry (1883–1967), served as the U.S. consul at Valparaiso, Chile; Nassau, Bahamas; Melbourne, Australia; Malta; and Port Elizabeth, South Africa.

ABRAHAM LINCOLN. His son, Robert Todd Lincoln (1843–1926), was U.S. Secretary of War (1881–85) and minister to Great Britain (1889–93).

Robert's wife, Mary Eunice Harlan (1846–1937), was the daughter of James Harlan, who was a senator representing Iowa and U.S. Secretary of the Interior (1865–66).

ANDREW JOHNSON. His daughter, Martha Johnson (1828–1901), married David Trotter Patterson (1818–91), a U.S. senator from Tennessee (1866–69).

Andrew's grandson—Martha's son—Andrew Johnson Patterson (1859–1932), was the U.S. consul in British Guiana.

ULYSSES S. GRANT. His son, Frederick Dent Grant (1850–1912), was the U.S. minister to Austria-Hungary (1889–93).

His son, Ulysses S. Grant, Jr. (1852–1929), was a delegate-at-large at the Republican National Conventions of 1896 and 1900, and a presidential elector-at-large in 1904 and 1908.

His daughter, Ellen "Nellie" Wrenshall Grant (1855–1922), married Frank Hatch Jones, her second husband, in 1912. He was the first Assistant Postmaster General under President Cleveland.

His sister, Mary Frances Grant (born in 1839), married Rev. Michael John Cramer, DD, who was the U.S. consul at Leipzig, Germany (1867–70), U.S. minister to Denmark (1871–81), and resident U.S. minister and Consul-General at Berne (1881–85).

JAMES ABRAM GARFIELD. His son, James Rudolph Garfield, was U.S. Secretary of the Interior (1907–09).

BENJAMIN HARRISON. His grandfather, William Henry Harrison, was President in 1841 (see above).

His son, Russell Benjamin Harrison (1854–1936), married Mary Angeline Saunders (1861–1944), whose father, Alvin Saunders, was a U.S. senator.

His grandson—Russell's son—William Henry Harrison (born in 1896), represented Wyoming in the U.S. House of Representatives three times: 1951–55, 1961–65, and 1967–69.

WILLIAM McKINLEY. His brother, David Allison McKinley (1829–92), was the U.S. consul in Honolulu and the Hawaiian Consul-General in San Francisco.

THEODORE ROOSEVELT. His daughter, Alice Lee Roosevelt (1884–1980), married Nicholas Longworth (1869–1931) in the White House in 1906. Longworth was Speaker of the House (1925–31).

His son, Theodore Roosevelt, Jr. (1887–1944), was Assistant Secretary of the Navy (1921–24), governor of Puerto Rico (1929–32), Governor-General of the Philippines (1932–33), and a posthumous winner of the Congressional Medal of Honor.

His son, Kermit Roosevelt (1889–1943), married Belle

Wyatt Willard (1892–1968), whose father, Joseph Edward Willard, was U.S. Ambassador to Spain.

His granddaughter, Nancy Dabney Roosevelt (born in 1923), married William Eldred Jackson, whose father, Robert Houghwont Jackson, was an Associate Justice of the U.S. Supreme Court.

His niece, (Anna) Eleanor Roosevelt (1884–1962), daughter of his brother Elliot (1860–94), married his fifth cousin, future President Franklin Delano Roosevelt. Theodore gave the bride away at the wedding in 1905.

His nephew, Theodore Douglas Robinson (1883–1934), son of his sister Corinne, was Assistant Secretary of the Navy.

WILLIAM HOWARD TAFT. His father, Alphonso Taft (1810–91), was Secretary of War for a few months in 1876, Attorney General (1876–77), U.S. minister to Austria-Hungary (1882–84), and U.S. Minister to Russia (1884–85).

His son, Robert Alphonso Taft (1889–1953) represented Ohio in the U.S. Senate (1939–53).

His grandson, Robert's son, William Howard Taft III (born in 1915), was U.S. Ambassador to Ireland (1953–57) and U.S. Consul-General at Loureno Marques, Mozambique (1960–62).

His grandson—Robert's son—Robert Taft (born in 1917), represented Ohio in the U.S. House of Representatives (1963–65 and 1967–71) and in the Senate (1971–76).

His great-grandson—William Howard Taft III's son—William Howard Taft IV (born in 1945), was Deputy Secretary of Defense (1984–89) and U.S. Ambassador to NATO (1989–92).

His half brother, Charles Phelps Taft (1843–1929), married Anne Sinton, whose father, David Sinton, was a member of the House of Representatives (1895–97).

WOODROW WILSON. His daughter, Jessie Woodrow Wilson (1887–1933), married Francis Bowes Sayre in 1913 in the White

House. Sayre was U.S. Assistant Secretary of State and High Commissioner to the Philippines.

His daughter, Eleanor Randolph Wilson (1889–1967), married William Gibbs McAdoo, who was U.S. Secretary of the Treasury (1913–18) and represented California in the U.S. Senate (1933–38).

HERBERT HOOVER. His son, Herbert Charles Hoover (1903–69), was U.S. Under Secretary of State (1954–57).

FRANKLIN DELANO ROOSEVELT. His fifth cousin, Theodore Roosevelt, was President (1901–09, see above).

His son, James Roosevelt (1907–91), was a member of the U.S. House of Representatives (1955–67).

His son, Franklin Delano Roosevelt, Jr. (1914–88), was a member of the U.S. House of Representatives (1949–55) and U.S. Under Secretary of Commerce (1962–65).

DWIGHT DAVID EISENHOWER. His son, John Sheldon Doud Eisenhower (born in 1922), was U.S. Ambassador to Belgium (1969–71).

His brother, Milton Stover Eisenhower (1899–1985), was appointed a personal representative of President Eisenhower with the rank of Special Ambassador on five occasions between 1953 and 1961.

JOHN F. KENNEDY. His father, Joseph Patrick Kennedy (1888–1969), was chairman of the U.S. Securities and Exchange Commission (1934–35), chairman of the U.S. Maritime Commission (1937), and U.S. Ambassador to Great Britain (1937–41).

His sister, Eunice Mary Kennedy (born in 1921), married (Robert) Sargent Shriver, Jr. (born in 1915), who was U.S. Ambassador to France (1968–70), and the Democratic candidate for Vice President in 1972.

His brother, Robert Francis Kennedy (1925–68), was U.S. Attorney General (1961–64) and then represented New York in the U.S. Senate (from 1965 until his death).

His nephew—Robert's son Joseph Patrick Kennedy II (born in 1952)—represented Massachusetts in the U.S. House of Representatives (1987–99).

His niece—Robert's daughter—Mary Kerry Kennedy (born in 1959), was married (1990–2003) to Andrew Cuomo (born in 1957), who was U.S. Secretary of Housing and Urban Development (1997–2001).

His sister, Jean Ann Kennedy (born in 1928), was U.S. Ambassador to Ireland (1993–98).

His brother, Edward Moore "Ted" Kennedy (born in 1932) has represented Massachusetts in the U.S. Senate since 1962.

His nephew—Edward's son—Patrick Joseph Kennedy (born in 1967), has represented Rhode Island in the U.S. House of Representatives since 1995.

GEORGE H.W. BUSH. His father, Prescott Sheldon Bush (1895–1972), represented Connecticut in the U.S. Senate (1953–63).

His son, George W. Bush (born in 1946), is President of the United States (2001–).

BILL CLINTON. His wife, Hillary Rodham Clinton, was elected senator from New York in 2000. She is the first First Lady to hold political office in her own right.

GEORGE W. BUSH. His father, George H.W. Bush, was President of the United States (1989–93, see above).

44

Presidents Who Were Related

OF THE FIRST 42 PRESIDENTS, FIVE PAIR SHARED LAST NAMES.

1. ADAMS: JOHN ADAMS (1797–1801) and JOHN QUINCY ADAMS (1825–29) were father and son.

2. HARRISON: WILLIAM HENRY HARRISON (1841) and BENJAMIN HARRISON (1889–93) were grandfather and grandson. William's son, John Scott Harrison, who served in the House of Representatives, was Benjamin's father.

3. JOHNSON: ANDREW JOHNSON (1865–69) and LYNDON BAINES JOHNSON (1963–69) were unrelated.

4. ROOSEVELT: THEODORE ROOSEVELT (1901–09) and FRANKLIN DELANO ROOSEVELT (1933–45) were fifth cousins. Theodore's paternal great(4)-grandparents, Nicholas Roosevelt (1658–1742) and Heyltje Kunst, were Franklin's paternal great(4)-grandparents. Theodore was descended through their second son, Johannes Roosevelt (born in 1689), while Franklin was descended through their third son, Jacobus Roosevelt (born in 1692).

5. BUSH: GEORGE H.W. BUSH (1989–93) and GEORGE W. BUSH (2001–) are father and son.

But far more Presidents were related to each other to one degree or another. They are noted below in order of the first presidential relative to hold office.

JOHN QUINCY ADAMS and BENJAMIN HARRISON were half-21st cousins, once removed, or 22nd cousins once removed. John's maternal great(20)-grandfather, Richard De Clare (1130–76), was Benjamin's paternal great(21)-grandfather. John was descended through his daughter Isabel De Clare (1171–1220) by his wife Eva MacMurrough (died in 1177), while Benjamin was descended through his son Roger "The Good" De Clare by his wife Alice De Meschines.

JOHN QUINCY ADAMS and THEODORE ROOSEVELT were 14th cousins, once removed. John's maternal great(13)-grandparents, John of Gaunt Beaufort (1340–98/9) and Catherine (or Katherine) Roet (1350–1403), were Theodore's maternal great(14)-grandparents. John was descended through their son Henry Beaufort (1367–1447), while Theodore was descended from their son Sir John Beaufort (1371–1410).

JOHN QUINCY ADAMS and GEORGE W. BUSH are 20th cousins, three times removed. John's maternal great(19)-grandparents, William Marshall (1170–1219) and Isabel De Clare (1171–1220), were George's maternal great(22)-grandparents. John was descended through their daughter Eva Marshall, while George is descended through their daughter Maud Marshall.

JAMES MADISON and ZACHARY TAYLOR were second cousins. James's paternal great-grandparents Col. James Taylor (1674–1729) and Martha Thompson (c1679–c1762) were also Zachary's paternal great-grandparents. James was descended through their daughter Frances Taylor (1700–61), while Zachary was descended through their son Zachary Taylor (1707–68).

MARTIN VAN BUREN and THEODORE ROOSEVELT were probably third cousins, twice removed. Martin's maternal great-great-grandparents were Luykas Gerritsen Wyngaart (c1645–1709) and Anna Janse Van Hoesen. Martin was descended from their daughter Elizabeth Wyngaart. Luykas and Anna appear to have had another daughter, Maria Wyngaart (born about 1685), who was Theodore's paternal great(4)-grandmother.

They were also third cousins, three times removed. Martin's maternal great-great-grandparents, Claas Gerritse Van Schaick, and his wife Jannetje, were Theodore's paternal great(5)-grandparents. Martin was descended through their son Laurens Van Schaick, while Theodore was descended through their son Emanuel Van Schaick.

WILLIAM HENRY HARRISON and JOHN TYLER were fourth cousins, once removed. William's great(3)-grandparents, William Armistead (1610–71) and Anne Ellis (born about 1615), were John's great(4)-grandparents. William was descended through their son John Armistead (c1640–c1703), while John was descended through their son Anthony Armistead (died about 1728).

WILLIAM HENRY HARRISON and ABRAHAM LINCOLN were fourth cousins. William's paternal great(3)-grandparents Thomas Harrison (1615–1682) and Katherine Bradshaw were Abraham's paternal great(3)-grandparents. William was descended from their daughter Hannah Harrison (1652–99), while Abraham was descended from their son Isaiah Harrison (1666–1738).

WILLIAM HENRY HARRISON and JIMMY CARTER are probably fourth cousins, five times removed. William's great-great-grandparents were Col. John Carter (1620–69) and Sarah Ludlow (born in 1629). Jimmy's paternal great(7)-grandfather was Thomas Carter, who appears to have been Colonel John's brother.

JOHN TYLER and BENJAMIN HARRISON were fifth cousins, once removed. John's great(4)-grandparents, William Armistead (1610–1671) and Anne Ellis (born about 1615), were Benjamin's paternal great(5)-grandparents. John was descended through their son Anthony Armistead (died about 1728), while Benjamin was descended through their son John Armistead (c1640–c1703).

MILLARD FILLMORE and GROVER CLEVELAND were fifth cousins, once removed. Millard's paternal great(4)-grandparents, John Post (1629–1711) and Hester Hyde (1625–1703), were Grover's paternal great(5)-grandparents. Millard was descended through their daughter Mary Post (1662–1705), while Grover was descended through their daughter Margaret Post (1653–1700).

Grover was also descended through John and Hester's other daughter, Sarah Post (born in 1659), the same number of generations. Margaret's grandson James Hyde (1707–93) married Sarah's granddaughter Sarah Marshall (1720–73).

FRANKLIN PIERCE and RUTHERFORD HAYES were fifth cousins, once removed. Franklin's great(4)-grandparents, Daniel Brewer (1596–1646) and Joanna Morrill (1602–88), were Rutherford's great(5)-grandparents. Franklin was descended through their son Daniel Brewer (1624–1708), while Rutherford was descended through their daughter Hannah Brewer (1630–1717).

FRANKLIN PIERCE and GEORGE H.W. BUSH are fifth cousins, four times removed. Franklin's great(4)-grandparents, Daniel Brewer (1596–1646) and Joanna Morrill (1602–88), were George's great(8)-grandparents. Franklin was descended through their son Daniel Brewer (1624–1708), while George is descended through their daughter Sarah Brewer (1638–1708).

Therefore, Franklin Pierce and George W. Bush are fifth cousins, five times removed.

FRANKLIN PIERCE and GEORGE W. BUSH are also fourth cousins, five times removed. Franklin's paternal great(3)-grandparents, Thomas Pierce (1618–83) and Elizabeth Cole (1614–88), are George's maternal great(8)-grandparents. Franklin was descended through their son Stephen Pierce (1651–1733), while George is descended through their son James Pierce (1659–1742).

Franklin and George are also second cousins, six times removed. Franklin's great-grandparents, Stephen Pierce (1679–1749) and Esther Fletcher (1681–1741 or 1742), were also George's maternal great(7)-grandparents. Franklin was descended through their son Benjamin Pierce (1726–64), while George is descended through their daughter Esther Pierce (born in 1711).

Some confusion arises here because Esther Pierce's daughter Esther Richardson (1727–1819) married James (1659–1742) Pierce's grandson Joshua Pierce (1722–71) in 1753, reuniting two branches as second cousins, once removed married.

ABRAHAM LINCOLN and BENJAMIN HARRISON were fourth cousins, twice removed. Abraham's paternal great(3)-grandparents, Thomas Harrison (1615–82) and Katherine Bradshaw, were Benjamin's paternal great(5)-grandparents. Abraham was descended from their son Isaiah Harrison (1666–1738), while Benjamin was descended from their daughter Hannah Harrison (1652–99).

ULYSSES GRANT and GROVER CLEVELAND were sixth cousins, once removed. Ulysses's paternal great(5)-grandparents, John Porter (1594–1648) and Anna White (1600–47), were Grover's great(6)-grandparents. Ulysses was descended through their daughter Mary (1637–81), while Grover was descended through their son Samuel (1635–89).

ULYSSES GRANT and FRANKLIN ROOSEVELT were third cousins, once removed. Ulysses's paternal great-great-grandparents, Lt.

Jonathan Delano (1648–1720) and Mercy Warren (born in 1658), were Franklin's maternal great(3)-grandparents. Ulysses was descended through their son Captain Jonathan Delano (1680–1752), while Franklin was descended through their son Thomas Delano.

ULYSSES GRANT and GEORGE H.W. BUSH are second cousins, four times removed. Ulysses's maternal great-grandparents, Samuel Weir (c1731–1811) and his wife Mary (died in 1790 or 1796), were George's maternal great(5)-grandparents. Ulysses was descended through their daughter Rebecca Weir (died about 1803), while George is descended through their son Jonathan Weir (c1755–c1832).

Therefore, Ulysses Grant and George W. Bush are second cousins, five times removed.

RUTHERFORD HAYES and GEORGE H.W. BUSH are sixth cousins, three times removed. Rutherford's great(5)-grandparents, Daniel Brewer (1596–1646) and Joanna Morrill (1602–88), were George's great(8)-grandparents. Rutherford was descended through their daughter Hannah Brewer (1630–1717), while George is descended through their daughter Sarah Brewer (1638–1708).

Therefore, Rutherford Hayes and George W. Bush are sixth cousins, four times removed.

JAMES GARFIELD and WILLIAM TAFT were fifth cousins, once removed. James's great(4)-grandparents, John Rockwood (1641–1724) and Joanna Ford, were William's great(5)-grandparents. James was descended through their daughter Joanna Rockwood (1669–c1710), while William was descended through their son Joseph Rockwood (1671–1713/23).

JAMES GARFIELD and GEORGE W. BUSH are fifth cousins, five times removed. James's maternal great(4)-grandparents, Walter Cook (died in 1695 or 1696) and his wife Catharine (died in 1695), are George's maternal great(9)-grandparents. James was descended through their son Nicholas Cook (1660–1730), while George is descended through their son John Cook (1635–1718).

BENJAMIN HARRISON and JIMMY CARTER are probably sixth cousins, three times removed. Benjamin's paternal great(4)-grandparents were Col. John Carter (1620–69) and Sarah Ludlow (born in 1629). Jimmy's paternal great(7)-grandfather was Thomas Carter, who appears to have been Colonel John's brother.

WILLIAM TAFT and RICHARD NIXON were seventh cousins, twice removed. William's maternal great(6)-grandparents, Ralph Hemingway and Elizabeth Hewes, were Richard's maternal great(8)-grandparents. William was descended through their daughter Elizabeth Hemingway, while Richard was descended through their son Joshua Hemingway (1643–1716).

WILLIAM TAFT and GEORGE H.W. BUSH are sixth cousins, three times removed. William's great(5)-grandparents, Thomas Davenport (1615–85) and Mary Pitman (1621–1691), were George's great(8)-grandparents. William was descended through their son John Davenport (1664–1724 or 1725), while George is descended through their son Jonathan Davenport (1658 or 1659–1728 or 1729).

Therefore, William Taft and George W. Bush are sixth cousins, four times removed.

Through another lineage, WILLIAM TAFT and GEORGE H.W. BUSH are eighth cousins, once removed. William's maternal great(7)-grandparents, Jonathan Fairbanks (1594 or 1595–1668) and Grace Lee Smith (died in 1673), were George's paternal great(8)-grandparents. William was descended through their son

George Fairbanks (1619–82), while George is descended through their son Jonathan Fairbanks (1628–1711).

Therefore, William Taft and George W. Bush are eighth cousins, twice removed.

WILLIAM TAFT and GEORGE W. BUSH are also fifth cousins, four times removed. William's maternal great(4)-grandparents, Peter Holbrook and Alice Godfrey, were George's maternal great(8)-grandparents. William was descended through their son William Holbrook (1693–c1776), while George is descended through their son Silvanus Holbrook.

HERBERT HOOVER and RICHARD NIXON were eighth cousins, once removed. Herbert's maternal great(7)-grandparents, Richard and Elizabeth Sawtell, were Richard's maternal great(8)-grandparents. Herbert was descended through their daughter Hannah Sawtell, while Richard was descended through their son Zachariah Sawtell.

45

Presidents Who Had All Their Children Live to See Them Take Office

1. ANDREW JACKSON (1829–37) had only one adopted son, Andrew Jackson, Jr. (1809–65), making him the first President to have "all his children" live to see him become President.

2. MILLARD FILLMORE (1850–53) was the first President to have all his biological children live to see his presidency. His son, Mil-

lard Powers Fillmore, was born in 1828 and died in 1889. His daughter, Mary Abigail Fillmore, was born in 1832 and died of cholera in 1854.

3. Ulysses S. Grant (1869–77). Four children: Frederick Dent Grant (1850–1912), Ulysses S. Grant, Jr. (1852–1929), Ellen "Nellie" Wrenshall Grant Sartoris Jones (1855–1922), and Jesse Root Grant (1858–1934).

4. Grover Cleveland (1885–89, 1893–97) did not have any of his children die before taking office, but then again, he didn't have any children before becoming President. He married Frances Folsom in 1886, and they had one child between his two terms, two children during his second term, and two children after he retired.

5. Theodore Roosevelt (1901–09). Six children: Alice Lee Roosevelt Longworth (1884–1980), Theodore Roosevelt, Jr. (1887–1944), Kermit Roosevelt (1889–1943), Ethel Carow Roosevelt (1891–1977), Archibald Bulloch Roosevelt (1894–1979), and Quentin Roosevelt (1897–1918).

6. William Howard Taft (1909–13). Three children: Robert Alphonso Taft (1889–1953), Helen Herron Taft Manning (1891–1987), and Charles Phelps Taft II (1897–1983).

7. Woodrow Wilson (1913–21). Three children: Margaret Woodrow Wilson (1886–1944), Jessie Woodrow Wilson Sayre (1887–1933), and Eleanor Randolph Wilson McAdoo (1889–1967).

8. Warren Harding (1921–23). One daughter: Elizabeth Ann Christian (1919–2005).

9. Calvin Coolidge (1923–29). Two sons: John Coolidge (1906–2000) and Calvin Coolidge (1908–24).

10. HERBERT HOOVER (1929–33). Two sons: Herbert Charles Hoover (1903–69) and Allan Henry Hoover (1907–93).

11. HARRY TRUMAN (1945–53). One daughter: (Mary) Margaret Truman Daniel (1924–2008).

12. LYNDON JOHNSON (1963–69). Two daughters: Lynda Bird Johnson Robb (born in 1944) and Luci Baines Johnson Nugent (born in 1947).

13. RICHARD NIXON (1969–74). Two daughters: Patricia Nixon Cox (born in 1946) and Julie Nixon Eisenhower (born in 1948).

14. GERALD FORD (1974–77). Four children: Michael Gerald Ford (born in 1950), John "Jack" Gardner Ford (born in 1952), Steven Meigs Ford (born in 1956), and Susan Elizabeth Ford (born in 1957).

15. JIMMY CARTER (1977–81). Four children: John "Jack" William Carter (born in 1947), James Earl "Chip" Carter III (born in 1950), (Donnell) Jeffrey Carter (born in 1952), and Amy Lynn Carter (born in 1967).

16. BILL CLINTON (1993–2001). One daughter: Chelsea Victoria (born in 1980).

17. GEORGE W. BUSH (2001–). Twin daughters: Barbara and Jenna (born in 1981).

46

Presidents Who Had All Their Siblings Live to See Them Take Office

1. JAMES MONROE (1817–25): sister Elizabeth Monroe (born in 1754), brother Spence Monroe (born in 1759), brother Andrew Monroe (1763–1836), and brother Joseph Jones Monroe (1764–1824).

2. ANDREW JOHNSON (1865–69): brother William Johnson (1804–65) and sister Elizabeth Johnson (born in 1806).

3. HERBERT HOOVER (1929–33): brother Theodore Jesse Hoover (1871–1955) and sister Mary "May" Hoover Leavitt (1876–1953).

4. HARRY TRUMAN (1945–53): brother (John) Vivian Truman (1886–1965) and sister Mary Jane Truman (1889–1978).

5. GERALD FORD (1974–77): half brother Thomas G. Ford (1918–95), half sister Marjorie King Werner (1921–93), half brother Leslie "Bud" Henry King (1923–76), half brother Richard A. Ford (born in 1924), half sister Patricia King (born in 1925), and half brother James F. Ford (1927–2001).

6. JIMMY CARTER (1977–81): sister Gloria Carter Spann (1926–90), sister Ruth Carter Stapleton (1929–83), and brother William "Billy" Alton Carter II (1937–1988).

7. RONALD REAGAN (1981–89): brother John Neil Reagan (1908–96).

8. GEORGE H.W. BUSH (1989–93): brother Prescott Sheldon Bush, Jr. (born in 1922), sister Nancy Bush Ellis (born in 1926), brother Jonathan James Bush (born in 1931), and brother William Henry Trotter Bush (born in 1938).

9. BILL CLINTON (1993–2001): half brother Roger Clinton (born in 1956).

47

The Three Presidents Who Fathered Children After Leaving Office

1. JOHN TYLER (1790–1862), who served from 1841 to 1845, was the first retired President to father children. He was also the first to marry while serving as President. Prior to his election, he and his first wife, Letitia Christian, had eight children between 1815 and 1830 (seven of them survived to adulthood). Letitia died a year and a half after Tyler became President. In June 1844 he married Julia Gardiner, 30 years his junior. After retiring from the presidency the following year, he and Julia went on to have seven children between 1846 and 1860: David Gardiner (1846–1927) was a congressman from 1893 to 1897, John Alexander (1848–83), Julia Gardiner (1849–71), Lachlan (1851–1902), Lyon Gardiner (1853–1935) was president of William and Mary College from 1888 to 1919, Robert FitzWalter (1856–1927), and Pearl (1860–1947).

2. Grover Cleveland (1837–1908), who served from 1885 to 1889 and then was reelected for the term 1893–97, was the second President to marry while in office. But unlike Tyler, that marriage was his first. He married Frances Folsom—who was his deceased law partner's daughter—at the White House in June 1886 (a month before her 22nd birthday), making her the youngest First Lady ever. Their first child, Ruth, was born in 1891, after he had retired from the presidency the first time. Esther and Marion were born in 1893 and 1895, during their father's second term. Following Cleveland's final retirement, Richard Folsom was born in 1897, and Francis Grover in 1903. Francis was the longest-lived of the Clevelands, dying in 1995.

3. Benjamin Harrison (1833–1901), who served from 1889 to 1893, married his deceased wife's niece Mary Scott Lord Dimmick in 1896. His two grown children (born in 1854 and 1858) objected to the marriage, but the retired President and the second Mrs. Harrison had a child, Elizabeth, in 1897.

48

The Two Presidents Who Fathered Children While in Office

1. Grover Cleveland (1885–89 and 1893–97) was the second President to marry in office, in 1886. Frances Folsom was 27 years his junior. Their first child, Ruth, was born between her father's two nonconsecutive terms, in 1891. Esther became the only child of a President to be born in the White House when she ar-

rived on September 9, 1893. Marion was also born during her father's second term, on July 7, 1895, in Buzzard's Bay, Massachusetts. Their younger brothers, Richard and Francis, were born after Cleveland retired from the presidency (1897 and 1903).

2. JOHN KENNEDY (1961–63), the youngest man to be elected President, took office at the age of 43. His wife, Jacqueline Lee Bouvier, was 12 years younger. They were married in 1953, the year he took his seat in the Senate. In 1956 they had a stillborn daughter. The following year, Caroline Bouvier—their only surviving child—was born. John Fitzgerald, Jr. followed in November 1960, two weeks after his father was elected President, but 56 days before he was inaugurated (he died in an airplane crash in 1999). On August 7, 1963, the Kennedys welcomed Patrick Bouvier—the third child to be born to a sitting President—who was born at Otis Air Force Base in Massachusetts. Patrick died two days after his birth, four months before his father was assassinated.

49

Presidents Who Were Firstborn Children

TWELVE OF THE PRESIDENTS WERE FIRSTBORNS.
1. JOHN ADAMS had two younger brothers: Peter Boylston (1738–1823) and Elihu (1741–76).

2. JAMES MADISON had eleven younger siblings: Francis (1753–1800), Ambrose (1755–93), Nelly Conway Madison Hite

(1760–1802), William (1762–1843), Sarah Catlett Madison Macon (1764–1843), Elizabeth (1768–75), Reuben (1771–75), Frances Taylor (1774–1823), and three siblings who died in infancy (1758, 1766, and 1770).

3. JAMES KNOX POLK had nine younger siblings: Jane Maria Polk Walker (1798–1876), Lydia Eliza Polk Caldwell Richmond (1800–64), Franklin Ezekiel (1802–31), Marshall Tate (1805–31), John Lee (1807–31), Naomi Tate Polk O'Harris (1809–36), Ophelia Clarissa Polk Hays (1812–51), William Hawkins (1815–62)—who served in Congress—and Samuel Wilson (1817–39).

4. ULYSSES GRANT had five younger siblings: Samuel Simpson (1825–61), Clara Rachel (1828–65), Virginia Paine Grant Corbin (born in 1832), Orvil Lynch (1835–81), and Mary Frances Grant Cramer (1839–1905).

5. WARREN HARDING had seven younger siblings: Charity Malvina Harding Remsberg (1867–1951), Mary Clarissa (1868–1913), Eleanor Priscilla (1872–78), Charles Alexander (1874–78), Abigail Victoria Harding Lewis (1876–1935), George Tryon, Jr. (1878–1934), and Phoebe Caroline Harding Votaw (1879–1951).

6. CALVIN COOLIDGE had one younger sister: Abigail Gratia (1875–1900).

7. HARRY TRUMAN had two younger siblings: (John) Vivian (1886–1965) and Mary Jane (1889–1978).

8. LYNDON JOHNSON had four younger siblings: Rebekah Luruth Johnson Bobbit (1910–78), Josefa Hermine Johnson White Moss (1912–61), Sam Houston (1914–78), and Lucia Huffman Johnson Alexander (1916–97).

9. GERALD FORD had six younger half siblings, three via his father Leslie Lynch King, and three via his mother Dorothy Ayer Gard-

ner King Ford: Thomas G. Ford (1918–95), Marjorie King Werner (1921–93), Leslie Henry King (1923–76), Richard A. Ford (born in 1924), Patricia King (born in 1925), and James F. Ford (1927–2001).

10. JIMMY CARTER had three younger siblings: Gloria Carter Spann (1926–90), Ruth Carter Stapleton (1929–83), and William "Billy" Alton II (1937–88).

11. BILL CLINTON has one younger half brother: Roger Clinton (born in 1956).

12. GEORGE W. BUSH had five younger siblings: Robin (1950–53), John Ellis "Jeb" (born in 1953), Neil Mallon (born in 1955), Marvin Pierce (born in 1956), and Dorothy Walker Bush LeBlond (born in 1959).

Presidents Who Were Last-Born Children

Seven of the Presidents were last-borns.

1. ANDREW JACKSON had two older brothers: Hugh (1763–79) and Robert (1765–81).

2. WILLIAM HENRY HARRISON had six older siblings: Elizabeth Harrison Rickman Edmonson (born in 1751), Anne Harrison Coupland (1753–1821), Benjamin VI (1755–99), Lucy Harrison Randolph Singleton (died in 1809), Carter Bassett (1756–1808; served in the House of Representatives, 1793–99), and Sarah Harrison Minge (1770–1812).

3. ANDREW JOHNSON had two older siblings: William (1804–65) and Elizabeth (born in 1806).

4. RUTHERFORD HAYES had four older siblings: Lorenzo (1815–25), Sarah Sophia (1817–21), Fanny Arabella Hayes Platt (1820–56), and a boy who died in infancy in 1814.

5. JAMES GARFIELD had four older siblings: Mehitabel Garfield Trowbridge (born in 1821), Thomas (born in 1822), Mary Garfield Larabee (1824–84), and James Ballou (1826–29).

6. FRANKLIN ROOSEVELT had one older half brother (from his father's first marriage): James (1854–1927).

7. RONALD REAGAN had one older brother: John Neil (1908–96).

Presidents Who Were Only Children

None of the Presidents were only children, although Franklin Roosevelt's one half brother was 28 years older than him, born to his father's first wife.

Not quites

George Washington (1789–97) had four older half siblings, born to his father's first wife, three of whom were alive at the time of his birth. He had five younger siblings.

50

The Five Presidents Who Didn't Live in the White House

THIS LIST DOES NOT INCLUDE THOSE VICE PRESIDENTS WHO SUC-ceeded to the presidency due to the death of a President, because their absence was, in most cases, a number of days, while the deceased President's family departed.

The White House, originally known as the President's House, didn't get the current name until it was repainted after the British burned it during the War of 1812. Its planning was begun during George Washington's term of office, and the cornerstone was finally laid on October 13, 1792 (while the national capital was still located in Philadelphia, though the move to what would be Washington, D.C., was planned). The building wasn't completed for another eight years.

1. GEORGE WASHINGTON (1789–97). When Washington was elected the first President, the national capital was in New York City. During his term of office, the capital was moved to Philadelphia, and land had been secured for what would become the capital city of Washington, D.C.

2. JOHN ADAMS (1797–1801). The second President began his term of office in Philadelphia, while the capital city was still under construction. The President's House took eight years to build, and was finally ready for the President's occupancy late in 1800. John Adams arrived on November 1, 1800.

3. JAMES MADISON (1809–17). On the night of August 24, 1814, the British entered Washington. A few hours earlier, the President had ordered a departure from the city, and ferried across the Potomac River. After touring the building and feasting on the uneaten dinner set in the dining room, the British set fire to the building. Rain a few hours later put the fire out, leaving the building just an empty shell. The Madisons returned to Washington on August 27, viewing the destruction the British had left. They lived for a time with Mrs. Madison's sister, and then moved to the Octagon, which had been the residence of the French minister. Rebuilding of the President's House began in March 1815, with the original architect, James Hoban, hired for the project.

4. JAMES MONROE (1817–25). When Monroe took office, recon-struction of the President's House was not yet finished. He and Mrs. Monroe stayed in temporary row-house quarters. Monroe insisted that it was necessary for him to reoccupy the house, and, though work was far from complete, several rooms were readied for occupancy. The Monroes moved into the President's House—which had by now been painted with the white-lead paint that would give it its name—in October 1817. The building was opened to the public on New Year's Day 1818 to show a re-turn to normalcy, and work was halted until February. This major reconstruction project was finally ended in January 1820.

5. HARRY TRUMAN (1945–53). The building was old and literally falling down in places, so upon returning from a trip in the au-tumn of 1948, the Truman family moved into Blair House, across the street from the White House. In 1949 the interior of the White House was completely demolished, leaving only the shell standing. It was shored up with steel, and new basements dug un-derneath. Then a new interior was built, though the work took longer than expected. But after a trip to Florida, Truman was al-lowed to return not to Blair House, but to the White House on March 27, 1952.

51

The Presidents' Fathers' Occupations

MOST OF THE PRESIDENTS' FATHERS HAD MULTIPLE OCCUPATIONS during their lifetimes. When the nation was founded, it was an agrarian society with the upper class also serving in public offices of one sort or another, so the first two categories are absolutely no surprise.

1. FARMER/PLANTER/LANDOWNER. Twenty-two of the 42 Presidents had fathers working the land in one way or another, including the first five Presidents' fathers, and 15 fathers of the first 16 Presidents—all except John Quincy Adams's father, John, who was a lawyer and the second President. The list of Presidents with farming fathers is: WASHINGTON, JADAMS, JEFFERSON, MADISON, MONROE, JACKSON, VAN BUREN, WHHARRISON, TYLER, POLK, TAYLOR, FILLMORE, PIERCE, BUCHANAN, LINCOLN, HAYES, GARFIELD, BHARRISON, COOLIDGE, TRUMAN, LBJOHNSON, and CARTER.

2. PUBLIC OFFICIAL. At least 16 of the Presidents' fathers served for some or most of their adult lives as public officials at some level of government. These range from local magistrates, sheriffs, and justices of the peace up to state governors, members of Congress, one ambassador (Kennedy's father, Joseph), and two Presidents (John Quincy Adams's and George W. Bush's fathers). The list of Presidents with fathers who served the public: JEFFERSON, MONROE, JQADAMS, WHHARRISON, TYLER, TAYLOR, PIERCE, AJOHNSON, BHARRISON, TAFT, COOLIDGE, KENNEDY, LBJOHNSON, CARTER, GHWBUSH, and GWBUSH.

3. MERCHANTS. Fourteen presidential fathers were merchants or salesmen of one type or another. These include: VAN BUREN, BUCHANAN, GRANT, HAYES, TROOSEVELT, COOLIDGE, HOOVER, TRUMAN, EISENHOWER, NIXON, FORD, CARTER, REAGAN, and CLINTON.

4 (tie). MILITARY. Ten Presidents' fathers served in the army or their state militia in some capacity, though none of them made a

career of it. The seven presidential fathers who served in uniform were: JEFFERSON, MADISON, VAN BUREN, TYLER, TAYLOR, PIERCE, LINCOLN, AJOHNSON, GHWBUSH, AND GWBUSH.

5 (tie). CRAFTSMAN/TRADESMAN. Seven Presidents' fathers were craftsmen of some sort, ranging from carpenters to leather tanners to mechanics. The seven were: JADAMS, MONROE, LINCOLN, GRANT, McKINLEY, HOOVER, and EISENHOWER.

Four presidential fathers had religious careers or ministries: AJohnson, Arthur, Cleveland, and Wilson. Four presidential fathers were lawyers: JQAdams, Tyler, Taft, and FDRoosevelt. And four of them were businessmen or financiers: FDRoosevelt, Kennedy, GHWBush, and GWBush.

52

The Presidents Who Died Before Their Parents

1. JAMES KNOX POLK. His mother, Jane Knox Polk, was born in 1776. She gave birth to her first child, the future President, in 1795, and then had nine more children, all of whom lived to adulthood. James represented Tennessee in the House of Representatives from 1825 to 1839. His younger brother, William Hawkins, also represented Tennessee in the House (1851–53). Jane lived to see her oldest son inaugurated as President in 1845. He retired after his one term in 1849. On the long journey to his new home after retirement, he became ill, and died on June 15,

1849, a scant three months after leaving office. He was the first President who did not outlive his mother; she died in 1852, having outlived seven of her ten children.

2. JAMES ABRAM GARFIELD. His mother, Eliza Ballou Garfield, was born in 1801, and had five children. Her youngest, James, was born in 1831. In 1881 she became the first mother of a President to attend his inauguration, and lived in the White House during his brief term. She died in 1888, having survived her assassinated President-son by seven years.

3. WARREN G. HARDING. His father, George Tryon Harding, was born in 1843. He enlisted, and was discharged for illness, twice during the Civil War. Later he went on to become a doctor. He had eight children, the oldest of whom, Warren, was born in 1865, and grew up to be President. George married three times: first, in 1863, to Harding's mother; then again at the age of 68; and finally at the age of 78. He lived to see his son inaugurated President, and lived to see him die in office in 1923. George died in 1928, making Harding the first President who did not outlive his father.

4. JOHN FITZGERALD KENNEDY. His father, Joseph Patrick Kennedy, was born in 1888; his mother, Rose Fitzgerald Kennedy, was born in 1890. His father was U.S. Ambassador to Great Britain (1937–40) and a successful businessman. His mother bore nine children—including one President (John), one Attorney General (Robert), and three senators (John, Robert, and Edward)—who in turn gave her more than 30 grandchildren (including several congressmen). The Kennedys were the first presidential parents to both outlive their President-son, who was assassinated in 1963. Joseph died in 1969, and Rose died in 1995, the longest-lived presidential parent ever.

George W. Bush's parents, President George H.W. Bush (born in 1924) and Barbara Pierce Bush (born in 1925), are only the third set of presidential parents to both see their son inaugurated President (after Grant and Kennedy). Barbara is the only woman to have lived in the White House as First Lady and visited her son there as the President's mother. All are still with us at this writing.

E PLURIBUS UNUM

THREE

RÉSUMÉ

The Presidents with Doctorates

ONLY ONE PRESIDENT EARNED A DOCTORATE: WOODROW WILSON, who got his Ph.D. in Political Science from Johns Hopkins in 1886. That was after he was admitted to the bar in North Carolina in 1882, and then gave up practicing law in 1883.

Five other Presidents did receive advanced degrees (all of them law degrees): Rutherford Hayes graduated from Harvard University Law School in 1845, was admitted to the Ohio bar in 1845; William Taft, University of Cincinnati Law School in 1880, Ohio bar, 1880; Richard Nixon, Duke Law School in 1937, California bar, 1937; Gerald Ford, Yale University Law School in 1941, Michigan bar, 1941; and Bill Clinton, Yale University Law School, 1973.

Franklin Roosevelt attended Columbia Law School from 1904 to 1907, but dropped out after passing the New York bar exam.

Fifteen more Presidents studied law and were admitted to the bar to practice as lawyers without attending specific law schools (for many of them, there were no specific law schools, and it was common for would-be lawyers to learn from practicing lawyers): John Adams (admitted to the bar in Massachusetts in 1758), Thomas Jefferson (Virginia, 1767), John Quincy Adams (Massachusetts, 1790), Andrew Jackson (North Carolina, 1787), Martin Van Buren (New York, 1803), John Tyler (Virginia, 1809),

James Polk (Tennessee, 1820), Millard Fillmore (New York, 1823), Franklin Pierce (New Hampshire, 1827), James Buchanan (Pennsylvania, 1812), Chester Arthur (New York, 1854), Grover Cleveland (New York, 1859), Benjamin Harrison (Ohio, 1854), William McKinley (Ohio, 1867), and Calvin Coolidge (Massachusetts, 1897).

54

Most Popular Pre-Presidential Jobs

A MAJORITY OF FUTURE PRESIDENTS SERVED IN THE MILITARY (SEE below), but for most it wasn't actually a career. Twenty-one future Presidents were lawyers, and the same number were members of their state legislatures. In descending order (the first two categories were equally popular):

LAWYER
The lawyers were: JAdams, Jefferson, JQAdams, Jackson, Van Buren, Polk, Fillmore, Pierce, Buchanan, Lincoln, Hayes, Arthur, Cleveland, BHarrison, McKinley, Taft, Coolidge, FDRoosevelt, Nixon, Ford, and Clinton.

STATE LEGISLATOR
The members of state legislatures were: Washington, JAdams, Jefferson, Madison, Monroe, JQAdams, Van Buren, WHHarrison, Tyler, Polk, Fillmore, Pierce, Buchanan, Lincoln, AJohnson, Garfield, TRoosevelt, Harding, Coolidge, FDRoosevelt, and Carter. Five served in Virginia, four in New York, three each in Massachusetts and Ohio, and two in Tennessee.

Washington and Jefferson were both in the Virginia House of Burgesses from 1769 to 1774. Jefferson and Madison were both in the Virginia House of Delegates from 1776 to 1777.

GOVERNOR OR EQUIVALENT
Nineteen future Presidents were governors of states or the equivalent: Jefferson, Monroe, Van Buren, WHHarrison, Tyler, Polk, AJohnson, Hayes, Cleveland, McKinley, TRoosevelt, Taft, Wilson, Coolidge, FDRoosevelt, Carter, Reagan, Clinton, and GWBush. Four of them were governor of New York, three of Virginia, and two each of Tennessee and Ohio. William Henry Harrison was the secretary of the Northwest Territory and the governor of the Indiana Territory; Andrew Johnson was the governor of Tennessee, and later the military governor of Tennessee; and William Howard Taft was the governor-general of the Philippines (1901–04).

REPRESENTATIVE
Eighteen future Presidents served in the U.S. House of Representatives. They were: Madison, Jackson, WHHarrison, Tyler, Polk, Fillmore, Pierce, Buchanan, Lincoln, AJohnson, Hayes, Garfield, McKinley, Kennedy, LBJohnson, Nixon, Ford, and GHWBush. Four represented districts in Ohio, three in Tennessee, and two each in Virginia and Texas. William Henry Harrison was the delegate from the Northwest Territory and later a Representative from Ohio. The other states that had future Presidents representing them in the House of Representatives were New York, New Hampshire, Pennsylvania, Illinois, Massachusetts, California, and Michigan. James Knox Polk was the only man to be both Speaker of the House and President, though Gerald Ford was House Minority Leader.

Madison and Jackson served in the House together from 1796 to 1797. William Harrison and Tyler were both in the House 1816–19. Polk and Buchanan were both in the House

1825–31. During the 1833–35 term, three future Presidents were representatives: Polk, Fillmore, and Pierce. Polk and Pierce continued together in the House until 1837, and Polk and Fillmore were in the House 1837–39. Lincoln and Andrew Johnson were in the House together 1847–49. Hayes and Garfield served together 1865–67. Garfield and McKinley were in the House together 1877–80. Kennedy, Lyndon Johnson, and Nixon were all in the House 1947–49. Kennedy, Nixon, and Ford served together 1949–50. Kennedy and Ford continued together until 1953. And Ford and George H.W. Bush were together in the House 1967–71.

SENATOR

Fifteen future Presidents served in the U.S. Senate: Monroe, JQAdams, Jackson, Van Buren, WHHarrison, Tyler, Pierce, Buchanan, AJohnson, BHarrison, Harding, Truman, Kennedy, LBJohnson, and Nixon. Two each represented Virginia, Massachusetts, Tennessee, and Ohio. The other states that had future Presidents representing them in the Senate were New York, New Hampshire, Pennsylvania, Indiana, Missouri, Texas, and California.

Jackson and Van Buren were both in the Senate from 1823 to 1825. Van Buren and William Henry Harrison were both in the Senate 1825–28 (Tyler joined them in 1827). Pierce and Buchanan were both in the Senate 1837–42. Lyndon Johnson and Nixon were both in the Senate 1951–53. Kennedy and Lyndon Johnson were both in the Senate 1953–61.

VICE PRESIDENT

Fourteen Vice Presidents later became President: JAdams, Jefferson, Van Buren, Tyler, Fillmore, AJohnson, Arthur, TRoosevelt, Coolidge, Truman, LBJohnson, Nixon, Ford, and GHWBush.

CABINET SECRETARY

Eight Cabinet secretaries (and two assistant secretaries) later became President: Jefferson (Secretary of State, 1790–93), Madison (State, 1801–09), Monroe (State, 1811–17, and War, 1814–15), JQAdams (State, 1817–25), Van Buren (State, 1829–31), Buchanan (State, 1845–49), Taft (War, 1904–08), and Hoover (Commerce, 1921–28). Theodore Roosevelt and Franklin Delano Roosevelt both served as Assistant Secretary of the Navy (Theodore, 1897–98; Franklin, 1913–20).

IN THE MILITARY

Twenty-nine Presidents served in the military before becoming President (13 in the army, six in the navy, nine in their state militias, and one military governor), but only three of them— William Henry Harrison, Ulysses S. Grant, and Dwight Eisenhower—were professional soldiers.

OTHER JOBS

Other shared pre-presidential jobs include: various local government positions (eight future Presidents served in government at the local or county level), ambassador (seven), teacher/professor (seven), some sort of federal appointment (six, ranging from local postmaster to Director of Central Intelligence), judge (four), various retail jobs (four), farmer/rancher (four), president of a university (four: the Eclectic Institute of Hiram, Ohio; the University of Cincinnati Law School; Princeton University; and Columbia University), businessman/entrepreneur (four), mayor (three), writer/reporter (three), and lieutenant governor (two).

55

Presidents Who Served in the Federal Government After Leaving Office

1. JOHN QUINCY ADAMS was President from 1825 to 1829. In 1802 he ran for, and lost, a seat in the House of Representatives. In 1803, however, he was appointed to the Senate to fill out an unexpired term, but was forced to resign (June 8, 1808) after breaking with his Federalist party to support President Jefferson's Embargo Act. In 1824 he ran for President as a Republican, and after a close election, the House of Representatives chose him as President over Andrew Jackson. In 1828 he lost his bid for reelection to Jackson, and intended to retire from public life. In 1830, however, he was persuaded to run for Congress and was elected to the House of Representatives as an Anti-Mason (he later became a Whig). He served a distinguished career in the House until his death in 1848 (he died in the Speaker's office).

2. JOHN TYLER finished out William Henry Harrison's one term as President, serving from April 1841 to March 1845, refusing to run for a term of his own. In February 1861 he was elected chairman of the Peace Convention in Washington, D.C., which tried to avert the oncoming Civil War. However, at the end of the

month he recommended that Virginia secede, and joined the Virginia Convention on Policy. In May he was elected to the Provisional Congress of the Confederacy, and late in the year, he was elected to the permanent Congress of the Confederacy (though he died before he was able to take his seat).

3. ANDREW JOHNSON served in the House of Representatives (1843–54) and the Senate (1857–62) before being appointed military governor of Tennessee (1862–64), and then replacing Hannibal Hamlin as Abraham Lincoln's Vice President in the election of 1864. After Lincoln's death, he succeeded to the presidency, and in 1868 became the first President to be impeached (on spurious charges). After his acquittal, he did not run for election to his own term, and retired in 1869. He ran unsuccessfully for the Senate in 1871 and the House in 1872, and then won election to the Senate in 1875. He took his seat, the only former President to serve in the Senate, on March 5, 1875, and then returned home, dying July 31, 1875.

4. ULYSSES S. GRANT was known as the general who won the Civil War, and after President Johnson appointed him Secretary of War *ad interim* in 1867, he was nominated for President by the Republican National Convention, and easily won the presidency, serving 1869–77. After his retirement, he sought nomination for a third term in 1880, but was defeated. Then he suffered several financial setbacks, and in March 1885, President Arthur returned him to the generals list with full pay ($13,500 a year). Grant died at the end of June.

5. WILLIAM HOWARD TAFT served as Theodore Roosevelt's Secretary of War (1904–08) and was Roosevelt's hand-chosen successor as President. He won the election of 1908, but Roosevelt's opposition (and candidacy for a third term) in 1912 propelled

Wilson into the presidency that year. Taft's early career as a lawyer, law school professor, and judge, seemed to point him more toward a judiciary career than the presidency, and the Supreme Court was his life's ambition. In 1921, President Harding appointed Taft Chief Justice, in which post he served until 1930. For health reasons, he resigned in February 1930, and died a month later, the only President to serve on the Supreme Court.

6. DWIGHT DAVID EISENHOWER, like President Grant before him, had his military rank restored after his retirement from the presidency. The Supreme Allied Commander during World War II, who was President from 1953 to 1961, was restored to his rank as General of the Army on March 22, 1961, by President Kennedy.

56

Former Presidents Who Ran for the Presidency After Leaving Office

THIS LIST DOES NOT INCLUDE SITTING PRESIDENTS WHO WERE defeated in their bids for reelection, but Presidents who had already left office and then decided to make a comeback.

1. MARTIN VAN BUREN (1837–41). In early 1841, the Missouri legislature nominated Van Buren to be their candidate for President in the election of 1844. By the time of the Democratic convention in 1844, Van Buren was the front-runner. He led on the first four ballots, but he wasn't able to gain the two-thirds of

the delegates necessary for nomination. James Knox Polk won the nomination (and the presidency). In 1848, abolitionist Democrats and antislavery Whigs combined to form the Free Soil Party, which nominated Van Buren for President (and John Quincy Adams's son Charles Francis Adams for Vice President). Van Buren didn't win any electoral votes, but did get about ten percent of the popular vote (about 291,000 votes), which was enough to swing the election from the Democrat (Lewis Cass) to the Whig (Zachary Taylor).

2. MILLARD FILLMORE (1850–53). While on a 13-month tour of Europe, Fillmore learned he had been nominated for President by the American Party (aka the Know-Nothing Party). He returned to the U.S. in June 1856, and also received the endorsement of the remnants of the Whig Party. In the election of 1856, Fillmore won 22 percent of the popular vote (about 875,000 votes), and carried the state of Maryland with its eight electoral votes. James Buchanan won the election, with John C. Frémont coming in second.

3. ULYSSES S. GRANT (1869–77). In 1880, Grant was the leading candidate for the Republican nomination. At the convention, he led on the first 35 ballots (coming within 66 votes of becoming the first President to be nominated for a third term). Eventually, however, James A. Garfield overtook him, taking the nomination and the presidency (and Grant's support).

4. GROVER CLEVELAND (1885–89). Cleveland lost his bid for re-election in 1888, losing to Benjamin Harrison (the grandson of former President William Henry Harrison). In 1892, Cleveland squeaked into the Democratic nomination on the first ballot. He went on to win 46 percent of the popular vote, to sitting President Harrison's 43 percent, and won the electoral vote 277 to

145, with 22 electoral votes going to People's Party (aka Populist Party) candidate James B. Weaver, making Cleveland the only former President to be elected President.

5. THEODORE ROOSEVELT (1901–09). When he was nominated for his own term in 1904, Roosevelt pledged not to run again in 1908. Instead, his handpicked successor, William Howard Taft, won the election of 1908. Late in Taft's term, Roosevelt grew concerned over the conservative direction his administration was taking, and declared his candidacy for the Republican nomination in February 1912. When he failed to take the nomination from Taft, Roosevelt left the party and ran on the Progressive, or Bull Moose, ticket. He actually came in second in the election of 1912. Wilson won 42 percent of the popular vote and 435 electoral votes; Roosevelt, 27 percent (88 electoral votes); sitting President Taft won 23 percent of the popular vote (eight electoral votes—he won only Utah and Vermont).

6. GERALD R. FORD (1974–77). Ford never ran for President after losing to Jimmy Carter in 1976, but in 1980 he considered (and was considered for) running as Ronald Reagan's Vice President. Negotiations for the ticket broke down when Ford demanded more of a co-presidency with Reagan, and Reagan chose George H.W. Bush as his running mate.

57

Vice Presidents Who Were Elected President

JOHN ADAMS

The first Vice President (1789–97) ran for the presidency when George Washington announced he would not seek a third term. In the election of 1796, Adams won 71 of the electoral votes to Thomas Jefferson's 68, making Adams the second President and Jefferson the second Vice President (in the first four elections, the candidate receiving the second greatest number of electoral votes became Vice President).

THOMAS JEFFERSON

The second Vice President (1797–1801) ran against the sitting President in the election of 1800, Jefferson as a Republican, Adams as a Federalist. Jefferson received 73 electoral votes to Adams's 65, but Aaron Burr, Jefferson's vice presidential candidate, also received 73 electoral votes. Because of the tie, it was up to the House of Representatives to decide the winner. The House took 36 ballots between February 11 and 17, 1801, before finally choosing Jefferson.

This deadlock and debate prompted passage of the 12th Amendment, providing for the election of the President and Vice President as a ticket. Jefferson and his new vice presidential candidate, George Clinton, won the election of 1804, defeating

Charles Pinckney (who had run as Adams's vice presidential candidate in 1800).

MARTIN VAN BUREN

After serving as Andrew Jackson's first Secretary of State, Van Buren replaced Vice President John C. Calhoun on the ticket in 1832, for Jackson's second term, and served as Vice President from 1833 to 1837. In 1837, Van Buren became the first sitting Vice President since Thomas Jefferson to run for the presidency, and the last to win it until George H.W. Bush in 1988. Van Buren received 170 electoral votes to William Henry Harrison's 73. Harrison would come back to defeat Van Buren in the election of 1840.

Van Buren made another comeback in 1848, running for President on the Free Soil ticket. He failed to win any electoral votes, but took enough of the popular vote (ten percent) to tip the election to Zachary Taylor over Lewis Cass.

THEODORE ROOSEVELT

After Vice President Garret Hobart died in office in 1899, Theodore Roosevelt was nominated for the spot when President William McKinley ran for reelection in 1900. Following McKinley's assassination in September 1901, Roosevelt became the youngest President ever (he was 42 years, 322 days old when he was inaugurated on September 14, 1901). In the election of 1904, Roosevelt was elected to his own term as President, winning 336 electoral votes to 140 for fellow New Yorker Democrat Alton Parker.

Roosevelt was the first Vice President to succeed to the presidency and then be elected in his own right. John Tyler succeeded William Henry Harrison in 1841, but wasn't nominated for his own term in 1844. Millard Fillmore succeeded Zachary Taylor in 1850, wasn't nominated in 1852, but did run on a third-party ticket in 1856, coming in third to James Buchanan and John C.

Frémont. Andrew Johnson succeeded upon Abraham Lincoln's assassination in 1865, but after his impeachment (and acquittal) he wasn't nominated for his own term. Chester Arthur succeeded upon James Garfield's death, but he too was unable to win nomination for his own term.

During the 1904 campaign Roosevelt pledged not to seek another term in 1908. He did, however, come back in 1912 to challenge William Howard Taft, his handpicked successor, giving the election of 1912 to Woodrow Wilson.

CALVIN COOLIDGE

Following Warren Harding's sudden death, Coolidge's father, a justice of the peace, swore him in as President on August 3, 1923. In 1924, Coolidge easily won the Republican nomination for his own term, and went on to defeat former ambassador John W. Davis and Senator Robert M. LaFollette (382 electoral votes, 136, and 13, respectively). Coolidge chose not to run for reelection in 1928.

HARRY S TRUMAN

John Nance Garner was Franklin Roosevelt's first Vice President, serving 1933–41. He unsuccessfully challenged Roosevelt for the presidential nomination in 1940, when Roosevelt chose his Secretary of Agriculture, Henry Agard Wallace, as his vice presidential running mate. At the Democratic convention in 1944, many delegates thought Roosevelt's declining health meant their choice for Vice President would be the next President and were unhappy with Wallace in that position. Roosevelt was forced to drop Wallace from the ticket, and chose Senator Truman to replace him. Less than three months into his fourth term, Roosevelt died, and Truman was thrust into the presidency.

Many delegates at the 1948 convention thought Truman was unelectable, but when the other choices withdrew their names from consideration, Truman was nominated on the first ballot.

He went on to win 49 percent of the popular vote and 303 electoral votes. He beat Thomas Dewey (45 percent, 189 electoral votes), Strom Thurmond (two percent, 39 electoral votes), and former Vice President Wallace (two percent, no electoral votes).

In 1949, Truman decided to not seek a third term as President, wanting to restore the custom of a two-term presidency. He announced this decision in March 1952. The 22nd Amendment—limiting the presidency to two terms, but specifically exempting Truman—was ratified in March 1951.

LYNDON BAINES JOHNSON

After running second to John Kennedy for the Democratic presidential nomination, Kennedy chose Johnson for Vice President. They narrowly defeated the Republican ticket of sitting Vice President Richard Nixon and Henry Cabot Lodge, 49.7 to 49.5 percent of the popular vote (303 electoral votes to 219, with 15 cast for Virginia Senator Harry F. Byrd). Following Kennedy's assassination on November 22, 1963, Johnson became President. He was nominated for his own term by acclamation of the Democratic National Convention in Atlantic City, New Jersey, and went on to defeat Barry Goldwater, 61 to 39 percent (486 electoral votes to 52). Johnson chose not to run for another term in 1968, although under the terms of the 22nd Amendment, he was still eligible.

RICHARD NIXON

Of the 14 Vice Presidents who later became President, only Nixon ran as a former Vice President. Nixon was Dwight Eisenhower's Vice President from 1953 to 1961. Inaugurated at the age of 40 years, 11 days, he was the second-youngest man ever to hold the office (John C. Breckenridge, Vice President from 1857 to 1861, was 36 years, 47 days old on inauguration day). Nixon ran for President in the election of 1960 but was defeated by John Kennedy. He lost the 1962 race for the governorship of California, and retired. Then he came back in 1968, narrowly won the Republican presidential nomination on the first ballot, and defeated sitting Vice President Hubert Humphrey and former Alabama Governor George Wallace in the election: Nixon 43.4 percent, 301 electoral votes; Humphrey 42.7 percent, 191; Wallace 13.5 percent, 46. He became the only former Vice President to be elected President.

In 1972, Nixon beat Senator George S. McGovern, 61 to 38 percent (520 electoral votes to 17) for the presidency, losing only Massachusetts and the District of Columbia. Facing almost certain impeachment for his activities surrounding the Watergate scandal, he became the first (and to date, only) President to resign, on August 9, 1974. President Ford pardoned him a month later.

GEORGE H.W. BUSH

Ronald Reagan went into the Republican National Convention with the nomination assured. Bush had been his closest challenger during the primaries, but couldn't muster enough support, and withdrew his name from consideration. At the convention, the greatest excitement came from behind-the-scenes negotiations to nominate former President Ford for Vice President, but the negotiations reportedly broke down when Ford wanted a commitment that he'd be more of a co-President. Instead, Reagan chose Bush as his running mate. They defeated Jimmy Carter's bid for reelection in 1980, and then former Vice President Walter Mondale in the election of 1984, winning 525 electoral votes in the latter election, the most ever.

In 1988, Bush easily won the Republican nomination, then beat Massachusetts Governor Michael Dukakis 54 to 46 percent (426 electoral votes to 111), becoming the first sitting Vice President to be elected President since Martin Van Buren in 1836.

In 1992, Arkansas Governor Bill Clinton blocked Bush's bid for reelection, taking 43 percent of the popular vote to Bush's 37 percent (independent Ross Perot won 19 percent). The electoral vote count was 370 for Clinton to 168 for Bush; Perot received no electoral votes.

58

Vice Presidents Who Succeeded to the Presidency But Were Not Elected to Their Own Terms

JOHN TYLER

William Henry Harrison won the Whig presidential nomination again in 1840, after having lost the election of 1836 to Martin Van Buren. Tyler was nominated for Vice President. This time Harrison defeated Van Buren, but he died of pneumonia on April 4, 1841, one month after taking office.

Having not been kept apprised of the President's health, Tyler was surprised when Fletcher Webster, the chief clerk of the Department of State, woke him early on April 5 to tell him of Harrison's death. Tyler was at home in Williamsburg, Virginia, and immediately left for Washington, where he was sworn in on April 6. As the first Vice President to succeed to the office of President, there was much debate over whether Tyler was acting President or actually President. He determined that he was indeed the President, and forced others to come around to his point of view.

In 1844, Tyler favored Democrat James Knox Polk over Henry Clay, who received his own party's nomination, so he refused to seek another nomination, and retired.

MILLARD FILLMORE

Fillmore ran as Whig Zachary Taylor's Vice President in 1848, and, due to the presence of former President Martin Van Buren running on the Free Soil ticket in the election, they were able to win 47 percent of the popular vote to Democrat Lewis Cass's 43 percent (Van Buren took ten percent), defeating Cass, 163 electoral votes to 127 (Van Buren didn't get any electoral votes). Fillmore visited the ailing President Taylor on July 9, 1850, and realized he was dying. Informed of Taylor's death late that evening, he was sworn in as President at noon on July 10. The Whigs refused to nominate Fillmore for his own term two years later, choosing instead Winfield Scott (who went on to lose to Democrat Franklin Pierce).

While on a 13-month excursion to Europe in 1855 and 1856, Fillmore learned that the American Party—also known as the Know-Nothings—had nominated him for President. He returned to the United States in June 1856 to accept the nomination, and won 22 percent of the vote (eight electoral votes), coming in third behind winner James Buchanan and John C. Frémont.

ANDREW JOHNSON

At the Republican convention of 1860, Abraham Lincoln was nominated for President on the third ballot, and Hannibal Hamlin was nominated for Vice President. In 1864, Hamlin was surprised he wasn't renominated. Lincoln chose Andrew Johnson—a southern Democrat who had remained loyal to the Union—for the second spot on his "National Union" ticket. When the tide turned in the Civil War during the campaign, the Democratic call for an immediate armistice looked like a mistake, and Lincoln won reelection 55 to 45 percent over George B. McClellan, 212 electoral votes to 21 (the 11 states of the Confederacy did not take part in the election). Lincoln was shot on April 14, 1865, and died early the next morning, thrusting Johnson into the presidency after little more than a month as Vice President.

In 1867, Congress passed—over Johnson's veto—the Tenure of Office Act, forbidding the President to remove anyone from his Cabinet without consent of the Senate. The measure was passed by the Republicans to attempt to control their non-Republican President. In February 1868, Johnson fired Secretary of War Edwin Stanton, who had been undermining his policies. On February 24, the House of Representatives voted to impeach Johnson, and in May he was acquitted by one vote. He served out the remainder of his term. At the ensuing Democratic convention of 1868, Johnson only received 65 votes on the first ballot, less than one-third of the total needed for nomination. Horatio Seymour eventually won the nomination, and Ulysses S. Grant the election.

CHESTER ARTHUR

Surprise candidate James Garfield was nominated on the 36th ballot at the Republican convention in 1880, wresting the nomination from former President Grant, who had been leading (but never by enough) through most of the convention. Chester Arthur was nominated for Vice President in an attempt to soothe hurt feelings over the presidential nomination. Garfield and Arthur barely defeated Winfield S. Hancock and William H. English, 48.3 to 48.2 percent (a difference of fewer than 10,000 votes out of nearly 9 million). Each ticket won 19 states, but Garfield/Arthur won the electoral college, 214 to 155.

On July 2, four months into his term, Garfield was shot. He died of his wounds two months later, on September 19. Arthur learned of the death about an hour later, at 11:30 P.M., and was sworn in about 2:15 the next morning by New York Supreme Court Justice John R. Brady. At that point there was no Vice

President, and since Congress wasn't in session, there was no President pro tem of the Senate, and no Speaker of the House. Had Arthur died then, there would have been no clear successor. To avoid such a catastrophe, Arthur drafted a proclamation calling the Senate into special session and mailed it to the White House. When he arrived in Washington, he was able to destroy the letter and call the Senate into session himself.

Arthur was briefly a candidate for his own term in 1884, but his change of heart on several issues virtually guaranteed that he would not be nominated at the Republican convention in 1884. James G. Blaine, who had been Garfield and Arthur's Secretary of State, won the nomination. Democrat Grover Cleveland won the election.

GERALD FORD

At the Republican National Convention in 1968, former Vice President Richard Nixon barely won the presidential nomination on the first ballot. Maryland Governor Spiro Agnew was nominated for Vice President. They won the election 43.4 to 42.7 percent (301 electoral votes to 191), with George Wallace running a distant third (he won 13.5 percent of the popular vote and 46 electoral votes). In 1972, they were renominated with only token opposition, then overwhelmingly beat the Democratic ticket of George S. McGovern and R. Sargent Shriver (61 to 38 percent). In October 1973, to avoid prosecution, Vice President Agnew resigned and pleaded no contest to one charge of income tax evasion. Under the terms of the 25th Amendment (ratified in 1967), Nixon nominated Ford for Vice President in November. The Senate confirmed him in November by a vote of 92–3, and the House did so in December 387–35. Ford was sworn in on December 6.

On August 9, 1974, minutes after Nixon's resignation, Ford was sworn in as President. A month later Ford pardoned Nixon, citing the need to save the country from what was expected to be a drawn-out, messy pretrial and trial should the former President be indicted. He chose Nelson Rockefeller as his Vice President, and he was confirmed in December 1974. In 1975, Rockefeller announced that he would not be a candidate for Vice President the following year. At the 1976 Republican National Convention, Ford was nominated for his own term on the first ballot, with 1,187 votes to 1,070 for Ronald Reagan. He chose Senator Robert Dole as his running mate, but they lost to Jimmy Carter and Walter Mondale, 50 to 48 percent (297 electoral votes to 240).

At the Republican convention in 1980, nominee Ronald Reagan briefly considered Ford for his vice presidential running mate, but the negotiations broke down when Ford demanded more of a co-President role. Reagan chose George H.W. Bush.

59

Political Parties to Which the Greatest Number of Presidents Belonged

1. REPUBLICAN. Eighteen Presidents served a total of 88 years between 1861 and 2008. After the party was formed in the 1850s (out of the remains of the Whigs, who had in turn come into existence when the Democrat-Republicans split into the Democrats and the Whigs), ABRAHAM LINCOLN was the first Republican to be elected President, in 1860. He was reelected on the "National Union" ticket four years later, with southern Democrat Andrew Johnson as his Vice President. Following Lincoln, the

Republicans became the dominant presidential party from 1869 to 1885 (ULYSSES GRANT, RUTHERFORD HAYES, JAMES GARFIELD, and CHESTER ARTHUR). Republican BENJAMIN HARRISON (1889–93) served in between Grover Cleveland's two terms, and then the Republicans resumed their dominance, with WILLIAM MCKINLEY, THEODORE ROOSEVELT, and WILLIAM HOWARD TAFT holding the office from 1897 to 1913. They again elected three in a row with WARREN HARDING, CALVIN COOLIDGE, and HERBERT HOOVER, from 1921 to 1933. DWIGHT EISENHOWER (1953–61) followed the Franklin Roosevelt/Harry Truman double decade. Next came RICHARD NIXON and GERALD FORD (1969–77), then RONALD REAGAN and GEORGE H.W. BUSH (1981–93), and most recently GEORGE W. BUSH, since 2001.

2. DEMOCRATIC. Fourteen Presidents served a total of 80 years between 1829 and 2001. In 1825 the Tennessee legislature renominated ANDREW JACKSON for President. In the election of 1828, Jackson's supporters called themselves Democrats, marking the evolution of Jefferson's Republicanism—as represented by the Democrat-Republicans—into what today we call the Democratic Party. Jackson's renomination in 1832 was the first in which candidates were chosen in a national party convention. Following his retirement, his Vice President (and handpicked successor) MARTIN VAN BUREN (1837–41) was elected. Then came JAMES KNOX POLK (1845–49), FRANKLIN PIERCE (1853–57), and JAMES BUCHANAN (1857–61). The Republicans dominated the office during Reconstruction, and the next Democrat to be elected was GROVER CLEVELAND, who won an election, lost an election, and then won an election, serving 1885 to 1889 and then 1893 to 1897. Four terms later, WOODROW WILSON (1913–21) was elected. With the coming of the Great Depression, FRANKLIN DELANO ROOSEVELT was elected four times (1933–45), followed by his vice presidential successor HARRY S TRUMAN (1945–53).

Eight years later, JOHN KENNEDY (1961–63) was the youngest man ever elected President, and after his assassination, LYNDON JOHNSON (1963–69) succeeded him and then was elected to his own term. Following the Watergate era, JIMMY CARTER (1977–81) was elected to one term, and then BILL CLINTON (1993–2001) rounded out the century.

3 (tie). DEMOCRAT-REPUBLICANS. Four Presidents served a total of 28 years between 1801 and 1829. The first truly contested election, in 1800, brought sitting Vice President THOMAS JEFFERSON into the presidency under the Democrat-Republican label. Jefferson, JAMES MADISON, and JAMES MONROE rounded out the "Virginia dynasty," serving 1801–25. JOHN QUINCY ADAMS also bore the D-R label, and served one term (1825–29) before the party split.

3 (tie). WHIG. Four Presidents served a total of eight years between 1841 and 1853. The Whigs only managed to elect two Presidents, but both of them died in office, with the result that there were in fact four Whig Presidents. WILLIAM HENRY HARRISON (1841) was the first President to die in office, and his successor, JOHN TYLER (1841–45), had to force the issue to be considered President, rather than merely acting President. ZACHARY TAYLOR won the election of 1848, but like Harrison, he died early, in 1850, and MILLARD FILLMORE (1850–53) succeeded to the presidency. After Fillmore was denied the nomination for his own term (and Winfield Scott lost the election), he was nominated in 1856 by the American Party (aka the Know-Nothings). The remnants of the Whigs then also nominated Fillmore, but his third-place showing marked the end of the Whigs as a party.

5 (tie). FEDERALISTS. Two Presidents served a total of 12 years between 1789 and 1801. GEORGE WASHINGTON's election as the first President was an uncontested affair. During his ·reelection in

1792, the Democrat-Republicans were growing in strength, but again Washington was uncontested and received all the electoral votes. JOHN ADAMS was his Vice President, and when Washington announced his retirement after two terms, Adams was the heir apparent. Having retired from Washington's Cabinet two years earlier, Thomas Jefferson mounted a campaign against Adams, but Adams squeaked out a victory, 71 electoral votes to 68, making Jefferson the Vice President.

5 (tie). NATIONAL UNION. Two Presidents served a total of four years between 1865 and 1869. ABRAHAM LINCOLN (1865; see Republican, above) and his second Vice President, ANDREW JOHNSON (1865–69).

60

The Five Presidents Who Ran for Office in Different Years for Different Parties

1. JOHN QUINCY ADAMS. As a senator representing Massachusetts in the first decade of the 1800s, Adams was a Federalist. In the election of 1824 (ultimately decided by the House of Representatives) party labels weren't used, but Adams was considered a Democrat-Republican, heir to the departing Virginia dynasty. By the election of 1828, the party was splitting, and Adams was known as a National Republican (though he lost the election to Andrew Jackson). The National Republicans evolved into the Whigs, and later into the modern Republicans.

2. MARTIN VAN BUREN. After serving as Andrew Jackson's Vice President, he was Jackson's chosen successor, received the Democratic nomination, and won the election of 1836. As a Democrat, he lost the election of 1840 to William Henry Harrison. In 1844 he was almost nominated again, but James Knox Polk took the Democratic nomination on the ninth ballot. In 1848 the abolitionist Democrats and antislavery, or "Conscience," Whigs joined forces to form the Free Soil Party, which nominated Van Buren for the presidency (former President John Quincy Adams's son Charles Francis Adams was the vice presidential candidate). They didn't win any electoral votes, but did take enough of the popular vote to swing the election to Whig Zachary Taylor.

3. MILLARD FILLMORE. Elected Vice President on the Whig ticket in 1848, he succeeded to the presidency upon Zachary Taylor's death. In 1852 the party nominated Winfield Scott instead. In 1856 the American Party, also known as the Know-Nothing Party, nominated Fillmore for President (the remains of the Whig Party then also nominated him). He came in third in the election, getting 22 percent of the popular vote and only eight electoral votes, and marking the end of the Whig Party.

4. ABRAHAM LINCOLN. He was the first Republican to win the presidency, in the election of 1860. The Republicans took the name "National Union" Party in the election of 1864, and Lincoln chose loyal southern Democrat Andrew Johnson as his running mate. Lincoln won reelection under the new name, becoming the only President to be elected under two different party labels.

5. THEODORE ROOSEVELT. After being elected Vice President in 1900, he succeeded to the presidency upon William McKinley's assassination in September 1901. He won election to his own term in 1904, but pledged not to run again. He chose his Secre-

tary of War, William Howard Taft, as his successor in the election of 1908. Taft won.

Disagreeing with Taft's policies, Roosevelt announced his bid for renomination in February 1912, but lost the nomination to Taft. He left the Republican Party, forming his own Progressive, or Bull Moose, Party. Under that banner, Roosevelt came in second in the election of 1912 (losing to victor Woodrow Wilson, but polling higher than Taft).

61

Presidents Who Served in the Military

TWENTY-NINE OF THE PRESIDENTS SERVED IN THE MILITARY, IN roles ranging from messenger and foot soldier to Commander in Chief and military governor. Thirteen served in the army (Washington, Monroe, Jackson, WHHarrison, Taylor, Pierce, Buchanan, Lincoln, Grant, TRoosevelt, Truman, Eisenhower, and Reagan), six in the navy (Kennedy, LBJohnson, Nixon, Ford, Carter, and GHWBush), nine in militias or national guard units (Madison, Tyler, Polk, Hayes, Garfield, Arthur, BHarrison, McKinley, and GWBush), and one as military governor (AJohnson).

GEORGE WASHINGTON was appointed a major in the Virginia militia in 1752, during the French and Indian War, but resigned his commission in 1754. He returned to service in 1755, and then was promoted to colonel and regimental commander. He resigned in 1758 to take his seat in the Virginia House of Burgesses.

In June 1775, he was a delegate to the Continental Congress when he was appointed Commander in Chief of the Continental Army. He led the army through the Revolutionary War, and resigned in November 1783, two months after the formal peace treaty was signed.

JAMES MADISON was commissioned a colonel in the Orange County (Virginia) militia in October 1775, but because of his frail health, saw no action and served only a brief time.

JAMES MONROE served in the Continental Army during the Revolutionary War, rising from lieutenant to major between March 1776 and December 1778, when he resigned his commission. In 1780, Governor Thomas Jefferson appointed Monroe military commissioner of Virginia with the rank of lieutenant colonel.

ANDREW JACKSON began his military career as a 13-year-old messenger in the Revolutionary War. In April 1781, he was captured by the British and spent two weeks in a prisoner-of-war camp in Camden, South Carolina, before being exchanged. Jackson was the last Revolutionary War veteran (and only prisoner of war) to be elected President. He was elected major general of the Tennessee militia in 1802, and appointed major general of the U.S. Volunteers by Governor William Blount of Tennessee in 1812. He served during the War of 1812, and was promoted to major general in the regular army in May 1814. He was a general during the First Seminole War (1817–18), served as military governor of Florida in 1821, and then resigned from the army.

WILLIAM HENRY HARRISON was a professional soldier from 1791 to 1798, serving in the Indian wars in the Northwest Territory. He joined up as an ensign with the First Infantry Regiment, was promoted to lieutenant in 1792, and then to captain in 1797. He resigned from the army in 1798. In 1812, he was commissioned a major general in the Kentucky militia, and then a brigadier general in the regular army in command of the Northwest frontier. In 1813, he was promoted to major general, but resigned in 1814 because of differences with Secretary of War John Armstrong.

JOHN TYLER served in the Virginia militia during the War of 1812, but saw no action.

JAMES KNOX POLK was commissioned a captain of a militia cavalry regiment in 1821, and later rose to the rank of colonel.

ZACHARY TAYLOR was a career military officer. He was commissioned a first lieutenant in 1808 and assigned to the Seventh Infantry Regiment, and promoted to captain in 1810. He served during the War of 1812, and was promoted to major in January 1815, but with the end of the war, he was reduced back to captain. He resigned in June 1815 to become a farmer, then rejoined the army as a major in 1816. He was promoted to lieutenant colonel in 1819, and to colonel in 1832. He commanded the First Infantry during the Black Hawk War (1832). In the Second Seminole War (1837–40), he commanded the Army South of the Withlacoochee, in Florida, and was breveted to brigadier general in 1838, taking command of all U.S. forces in Florida. He also served during the Mexican War (1846–48), but had major disagreements with President Polk over his actions. He retired as a major general in 1848.

MILLARD FILLMORE organized the Union Continentals—the Buffalo home guard—at the outbreak of the Civil War, some eight years after he retired from the presidency.

FRANKLIN PIERCE served during the Mexican War (1846–48). He enlisted as a private in the Concord, New Hampshire, volunteers in May 1846, was commissioned a colonel in the regular army in February 1847, promoted to brigadier general the next month, and resigned from the army in 1848.

JAMES BUCHANAN served briefly in the Third Cavalry in 1814, during the War of 1812.

ABRAHAM LINCOLN enlisted in the Illinois volunteers in 1832, during the Black Hawk War, and was elected captain of his company of volunteers. He served three months and saw no action.

ANDREW JOHNSON was appointed Military Governor of Tennessee, with the rank of brigadier general, by President Lincoln on March 4, 1862. He served in this post until he was elected Vice President in 1864.

ULYSSES GRANT was a professional soldier, the first graduate of a military academy (West Point in 1843) to be elected President. Upon his graduation, he was commissioned a brevet second lieutenant and assigned to the Fourth Infantry. The commission was made permanent in 1845. He served during the Mexican War (1846–48), and was promoted to first lieutenant in September 1847. In 1853, he was promoted to captain, but resigned in 1854 to take up farming with his family.

At the outbreak of the Civil War, Grant requested recommission in the army, but never received a reply. He was appointed colonel of the 21st Illinois Infantry in June 1861, promoted to brigadier general two months later, and then to major general in February 1862. In November 1863, he was promoted to lieutenant general, and became commander of all Union armies in March 1864. In July 1866, he was promoted to general of the army, the first to hold that rank since Washington. He served as Secretary of War *ad interim* from 1867 to 1868.

After his presidency, Grant faced severe financial difficulties. In early 1885, facing death from cancer, Congress restored his rank as general with full pay.

RUTHERFORD HAYES served in the 23rd Ohio Volunteer Infantry Regiment during the Civil War. He was commissioned a major in June 1861. In October, he was promoted to lieutenant colonel and deputy commander of the regiment. He was severely wounded in September 1862 while serving as acting commander of the regiment. In October, he was promoted to colonel and commander of the regiment. In October 1864, he was again wounded, and then promoted to brigadier general of volunteers. In March 1865, he was breveted to major general, and resigned in June.

JAMES GARFIELD served in the Union Army during the Civil War. He was commissioned a lieutenant colonel in the Ohio 42nd Regiment in August 1861, and promoted to colonel in November. He was promoted to brigadier general in early 1862, appointed chief of staff of the Army of the Cumberland in January 1863, and promoted to major general in late 1863. Garfield was elected to the House of Representatives in September 1862, and resigned from the army in December 1863 to take his seat in Congress.

CHESTER ARTHUR served in the New York State militia from February 1858 to December 1862, rising from brigade judge advocate to quartermaster general. In January 1861, he was appointed engineer in chief with the rank of brigadier general. In April, he was promoted to acting assistant quartermaster general. In February 1862, he became inspector general, and in July, quartermaster general.

BENJAMIN HARRISON served with the 70th Indiana Infantry Regiment during the Civil War. He rose from second lieutenant to brigadier general between July 1862 and June 1865.

WILLIAM MCKINLEY served with the 23rd Ohio Volunteer Infantry during the Civil War. He enlisted as a private in June 1861, and first saw action in September. In April 1862, he was promoted to commissary sergeant. For extreme valor, he was promoted to second lieutenant in September 1862, placed in command of Company D, and appointed to the staff of Colonel Rutherford B. Hayes (see above). In February 1863, McKinley was promoted to first lieutenant, and to captain in July. In March 1865, he was promoted to brevet major. He left the service in July, having never been wounded.

THEODORE ROOSEVELT was a member of the New York National Guard from 1882 to 1885, rising from second lieutenant to captain. From May to September 1898, during the Spanish-American War, he commanded the First U.S. Volunteer Cavalry Regiment, popularly known as the "Rough Riders." He was promoted to colonel for his actions. During World War I, after his presidency, he offered to raise a force of volunteers, but President Wilson denied the request.

HARRY TRUMAN served in the Missouri National Guard from 1905 to 1911, and then rejoined in May 1917. His unit became part of the regular army during World War I, and he served with the 129th Field Artillery from August 1917 to May 1919, rising from lieutenant to major. He was neither wounded nor decorated.

DWIGHT EISENHOWER was a professional soldier, the second graduate of West Point to become President. He graduated 61st of 164 in the class of 1915. Upon graduation, he was commissioned a second lieutenant and assigned to the 19th Infantry. He was promoted to first lieutenant in July 1916, and to captain in May 1917. During World War I, he served as an instructor in the United States, and received temporary wartime promotions to major in June 1917, and to lieutenant colonel in October 1918. After the war, he resumed his rank of captain, and was promoted to major in June 1920.

Eisenhower attended Command and General Staff School from 1925 to 1926, and the Army War College from 1928 to 1929. He served as special assistant to the Secretary of War from 1929 to 1932. He was promoted to lieutenant colonel in July 1936 while serving on General MacArthur's staff in the Philippines, to colonel in March 1941, and then to brigadier general six months later. When the United States entered World War II, he was chief of staff to III Corps Commander General Walter Krueger, and then became assistant chief of staff in charge of plans in Washington.

In March 1942, he was promoted to major general and named chief of the general staff's operations division. In June, he was appointed commander of U.S. forces in Europe, and promoted in July to lieutenant general. In February 1943, Eisenhower was promoted to general, and in December, President Roosevelt named him Supreme Allied Commander with orders to invade Europe. In December 1944 he was promoted to five-star general. He accepted Germany's surrender in May 1945, and in November, became Army Chief of Staff.

Eisenhower resigned from the army in February 1948, and became president of Columbia University. In December 1950, President Truman appointed Eisenhower Supreme Commander of the North Atlantic Treaty Organization (NATO), and he assumed the post in April 1951. He resigned from NATO in May 1952, and from the army in July, following his nomination for President.

JOHN KENNEDY served in the U.S. Navy from September 1941 to April 1945. He had volunteered for the army, but was refused because of his bad back. In the navy, he rose from ensign to lieutenant. Through his father's influence, he got a sea command of *PT-109*. His boat was rammed in the Solomon Islands on August 2, 1943, and due to his later actions, he was awarded the Navy and Marine Corps Medal. Kennedy was the first navy veteran to become President.

LYNDON JOHNSON joined the naval reserve in January 1940, and served as a lieutenant commander in the navy from December 1941 to July 1942. He received the Silver Star for an observation mission over New Guinea when his plane was attacked by Japanese aircraft. He resigned his commission in 1942 to comply with President Roosevelt's order that all congressmen in the service resume their legislative duties (Johnson had first been elected to the House of Representatives in 1936, and retained his seat during his military service).

RICHARD NIXON joined the navy in June 1942 and underwent basic training in Rhode Island (where he met William P. Rogers, his future Secretary of State). He started out as a lieutenant junior grade, and was an aide at the Naval Reserve Air Base in Ottumwa, Iowa, from October 1942 to May 1943, before shipping out to the South Pacific. He was the officer in charge of the South Pacific Combat Air Transport Command at Bougainville and Green Island from January to June 1944, and was cited for "meritorious and efficient performance." From December 1944, he was assigned to the Navy Department's Bureau of Aeronautics in Washington, and left the navy in March 1946 a lieutenant commander.

GERALD FORD joined the navy in April 1942 and underwent basic training at the Naval Academy in Annapolis. As an ensign, he was made a physical fitness instructor at a preflight school in North Carolina, but requested sea duty in 1943, and was assigned to the USS *Monterey* as athletic director and gunnery division officer. He later was made assistant navigator. Ford received ten battle stars during his service, and finished out his time at the Naval Reserve Training Command at Glenview, Illinois. He retired from the navy a lieutenant commander in February 1946.

JIMMY CARTER was the first Naval Academy graduate to become President. He had sea duty in 1944 aboard the USS *New York*, and graduated 59th of 820 in the wartime class of 1947 (which was graduated in June 1946). After being commissioned as an ensign, he served as an electronics instructor aboard the USS *Wyoming* and USS *Mississippi*. In 1948, he attended submarine school in New London, Connecticut, and graduated third of 52 in December 1948. He was assigned to the submarine *Pomfret*, and then reassigned to the antisub submarine *K-1* in 1950. Carter joined the nuclear submarine program in 1951, and studied nuclear physics at Union College in Schenectady, New York. He then served as engineering officer aboard the *Sea Wolf.* He resigned from the navy in 1953 to take over the family farming business after his father's death.

RONALD REAGAN was a second lieutenant in the Army Reserve, and called up to active duty following U.S. entry into World War II. His poor eyesight barred him from combat, so his first assignment was loading convoys at Fort Mason in San Francisco, California. He was transferred to the Army Air Force First Motion Picture Unit, and narrated preflight training films for bomber pilots about to conduct raids over Japan. While in the service, he appeared in Irving Berlin's musical film *This Is the Army* (1943). He left the army in July 1945 as a captain.

GEORGE H.W. BUSH enlisted in the navy on his 18th birthday, June 12, 1942, as a seaman second class. He underwent flight training, and earned his wings and a commission as an ensign in June 1943, becoming the youngest pilot in the navy. He flew 58 combat missions in a Grumman Avenger off the carrier *San Jacinto* as part of VT-51. On June 19, 1944, he crash-landed in the sea, and was rescued by the USS *Bronson*. On September 2, 1944, his plane was hit during a mission against Chichi Jima in the Bonin Islands. After completing the mission, he bailed out of the crashing airplane, was rescued by the submarine *Finback*, and received the Distinguished Flying Cross. He left the navy in September 1945 as a lieutenant (junior grade).

GEORGE W. BUSH served in the Texas Air National Guard from 1968 to 1974, although his service during the entire period was questioned during his presidential campaigns.

62

The Three Presidents Who Graduated from Military Academies

ONLY THREE PRESIDENTS WERE GRADUATES OF U.S. MILITARY academies.

1. ULYSSES S. GRANT, West Point, class of 1843. In 1838, without Grant's knowledge, his father arranged for Representative Thomas L. Hamer to appoint him to West Point. Grant was scared that he would flunk out, but entered the academy in May 1839. He excelled at math and horsemanship, and set a high-jump record on horseback, but had more difficulty with most of his other subjects. He graduated 21st in his class of 39, and requested assignment to the dragoons (cavalry). His excellent horsemanship was deemed not enough to make up for his poor class standing, and he was commissioned a brevet second lieutenant in the infantry.

2. DWIGHT D. EISENHOWER, West Point, class of 1915 (also attended Command and General Staff School, 1925–26, and Army War College, 1928–29). Eisenhower took the entrance exam for the U.S. Naval Academy, but he was too old to be accepted, hav-

ing passed his twentieth birthday. He settled for West Point, and was an average student. His best subjects were engineering, ordnance, gunnery, drill regulation, and athletics. He was a star halfback on the football team, but sustained a major knee injury in a game against Tufts in 1912, and was barred from playing football afterward. He wound up coaching the junior varsity squad. The future President ranked 57 of 212 at the end of his first year, 81 of 177 at the end of the second, 65 of 170 after three years, and graduated 61st of 164. Upon graduation, he was commissioned a second lieutenant and assigned to the 19th Infantry.

3. Jimmy Carter, Annapolis, class of 1946 (also attended submarine school, 1948, and studied nuclear physics at Union College, Schenectady, New York, 1951). In 1941, Carter attended Georgia Southwestern College in Americus, Georgia. He applied to the U.S. Naval Academy, took additional math courses at Georgia Institute of Technology in 1942, and was admitted to Annapolis in 1943. His best subjects were electronics, gunnery, and naval tactics. During 1944, he had sea duty aboard the USS *New York* on East Coast–Caribbean patrol. He graduated 59th of 820 in the accelerated wartime class of 1947 that graduated in June 1946. He was commissioned an ensign, and served as an electronics instructor aboard the USS *Wyoming* and USS *Mississippi* starting in 1946. Carter rose to lieutenant senior grade by 1953, and then resigned from the navy to manage the family farming business following his father's death.

63

Presidents Who Ran Unsuccessfully for the Presidency Before Their Election

1. JOHN ADAMS (1797–1801). Before the passage of the 12th Amendment, the Vice President was the candidate who received the second-most electoral votes for President. John Adams came in second in the first two elections (1789 and 1792), and, as the loser, served as George Washington's Vice President.

2. THOMAS JEFFERSON (1801–09). Upon George Washington's retirement, John Adams was the de facto Federalist candidate. Jefferson, having resigned from Washington's Cabinet in 1793, was free to run against Adams, and did so as a Democrat-Republican in 1796. He received the second-greatest number of electoral votes and thus was the Vice President.

3. JOHN QUINCY ADAMS (1825–29). Not a formal candidate, Adams received one electoral vote, from Governor William Plumer of New Hampshire, in the election of 1820 (James Monroe's reelection). According to legend, Plumer voted for Adams "so that Washington would remain the only President unanimously chosen by the electoral college." Other sources, however, show that Plumer genuinely disliked Monroe, and voted against him in earnest.

4. ANDREW JACKSON (1829–37). By the election of 1824, the nominating caucus had died out, but national nominating conventions had not yet appeared. Retiring Secretary of State John Quincy Adams was nominated by the Massachusetts legislature, and had the backing of New England in his quest for the presidency. Tennessee's Andrew Jackson was nominated by his state legislature in August 1822, and was the most popular candidate in the campaign. But the presence of Kentucky's Henry Clay and Georgia's William H. Crawford in the race virtually guaranteed that no candidate would be able to amass a majority. The popular vote totals were: Jackson, 155,872; Adams, 105,321; Clay, 46,587; and Crawford, 44,282. The electoral college votes went to Jackson (99), Adams (84), Crawford (41), and Clay (37), throwing the election to the House of Representatives. The 12th Amendment directed the House to choose from among the top three electoral vote recipients, knocking Clay out of consideration. Clay gave his support to Adams, and on February 9, 1825, the House voted by state for President. Adams won 13 states, Jackson took seven, and Crawford four.

5. WILLIAM HENRY HARRISON (1841). In 1834, opposition to President Andrew Jackson was coalescing into what became known as the Whig Party. But the Whigs were too disorganized to nominate and support a single candidate against Jackson's chosen successor, Vice President Martin Van Buren, in the election of 1836. Instead, the Whigs nominated three candidates, each popular in his own region, hoping to have the House of Representatives again choose the President. Pennsylvania nominated Harrison as the candidate of the West, Massachusetts chose Daniel Webster as the candidate of the Northeast, and Tennessee chose Hugh Lawson White as the candidate of the South. The Whig strategy failed. Van Buren received 51 percent of the popular vote to Harrison's 36 percent (White took ten and Webster

three percent). In the electoral college, Van Buren got 170 votes to Harrison's 73 (White had 26, Webster 14, and undeclared candidate Willie P. Mangum of North Carolina received 11).

6. GROVER CLEVELAND (1885–89, 1893–97). Cleveland won the election of 1884, which was very close. He won the popular vote by less than two-thirds of one percent (popular vote, 4,911,017 to 4,848,334; electoral vote, 219 to 182), defeating Maine's James G. Blaine. Cleveland was then defeated in his bid for reelection by Benjamin Harrison, losing by less than one percent of the popular vote (5,540,329 to 5,439,853; 233 to 168 electoral votes). The election of 1892 had a more creditable third-party candidate (James B. Weaver of the People's Party), and Cleveland defeated Harrison easily (5,556,918 to 5,176,108, with 1,041,028 votes for Weaver; electoral vote, 277 to 145 to 22).

7. RICHARD NIXON (1969–74). Nixon was Eisenhower's Vice President from 1953 to 1961, and the Republican nominee for President in 1960. He lost the remarkably close election of 1960 to young, photogenic, Massachusetts senator John Kennedy. (The popular vote was 34,227,096 to 34,108,546, the electoral vote, 303 to 219; noncandidate Senator Harry F. Byrd of Virginia received 15 electoral votes from Alabama and Mississippi.) The 118,000-vote difference represented less than 0.2 percent of the popular vote. Nixon then lost his bid to become governor of California in 1962, and in a celebrated postelection news conference, announced: "You won't have Nixon to kick around anymore, because, gentlemen, this is my last press conference."

64

Presidents Who Previously Served in the Cabinet

1. THOMAS JEFFERSON (1801–09) was the first Secretary of State, serving from 1790 to 1793. He organized the department, but clashed frequently with Secretary of the Treasury Alexander Hamilton. Jefferson resigned when it became clear to him that Washington was favoring Hamilton's views.

2. JAMES MADISON (1809–17) was Thomas Jefferson's Secretary of State, serving the full eight years (1801–09). Madison supported the Louisiana Purchase, encouraged resistance to the tribute the Barbary Pirates demanded, and urged an embargo against Britain and France in retaliation for their harassment of U.S. ships (and especially for British impressment). Madison was Jefferson's chosen successor for the presidency.

3. JAMES MONROE (1817–25) was Madison's second Secretary of State, serving from 1811 to 1817. As Secretary, he could not find a peaceful solution to the problems with Great Britain, and concluded that war would be less injurious than the current state of affairs between the nations. He ordered the evacuation of all important papers from the State Department in advance of the British invasion of Washington in 1814. After the British withdrawal, he was appointed Secretary of War by Madison and was military commander of the Federal District (concurrent with his

duties as Secretary of State). He was Madison's third Secretary of War, serving 1814–15, and though unable to convince Congress of the need for a draft, was able to strengthen the army by offering greater inducements for service. He was Madison's heir apparent, and won the presidency in 1816.

4. JOHN QUINCY ADAMS (1825–29) was Monroe's Secretary of State for all eight years. He negotiated the Convention of 1818 with Britain, establishing the U.S.-Canadian border from Minnesota to the Rocky Mountains. He concluded the Adams-Onís Treaty with Spain in 1819, transferring Spanish Florida to the United States, fixing the southern boundary of the United States, and removing Spanish claims to Oregon. And he was instrumental in the form and content of the Monroe Doctrine.

5. MARTIN VAN BUREN (1837–41) was Andrew Jackson's first Secretary of State, serving from 1829 to 1831. He negotiated a commercial treaty with Turkey in 1830, gaining navigation rights on the Black Sea for the United States. Also in 1830, he negotiated a treaty with Great Britain, renewing U.S. rights to trade with the West Indies. And he helped win reparations from France for losses incurred during the Napoleonic Wars. He resigned in 1831 to help Jackson with an overall Cabinet shake-up. Jackson named Van Buren minister to Great Britain, but the Senate rejected the nomination. In 1832, Van Buren was elected Jackson's Vice President.

6. JAMES BUCHANAN (1857–61) was James Polk's Secretary of State from 1845 to 1849. Polk directed most foreign policy himself, limiting Buchanan's influence. Buchanan did make the final arrangements for the annexation of Texas, however, and negotiated the 1846 Oregon Treaty with Great Britain, fixing the U.S.-Canadian border in the far West at the 49th parallel (giving present-day Washington and Oregon to the United States, and all of Vancouver Island to Canada).

7. WILLIAM HOWARD TAFT (1909–13) served as Theodore Roosevelt's second Secretary of War (1904–08). He supervised preparations for the construction of the Panama Canal, personally inspecting the site in November and December 1904. In July 1905, Taft met with Japanese Premier Count Taro Katsura, and assured Katsura that the United States would not oppose the Japanese taking over Korea, as long as it was not a prelude to aggression against the Philippines; Roosevelt approved the deal after the fact. Taft was in the Philippines from July to September 1905. He was the provisional governor of Cuba during September and October 1906. Taft also served as acting Secretary of State during John Hay's final illness (he died in office in 1905). Roosevelt endorsed Taft to succeed him as President, and Taft resigned from the Cabinet in order to campaign for the presidency.

8. HERBERT HOOVER (1929–33) was Secretary of Commerce under Harding and Coolidge, serving from 1921 to 1928. Hoover was very active in his post, expanding the Bureau of Standards and the amount of data collected by the Census Bureau. He established the Aeronautics Board under the Air Commerce Act of 1926, started the regulation of the airwaves under the Radio Act of 1927, worked to increase food exports, improved the nation's inland waterways, and persuaded the steel industry to abandon the 12-hour workday. He pushed for the construction of the St. Lawrence Seaway, and of the Boulder Dam (which was later renamed in his honor). He was a candidate for the vice presidential nomination in 1924, but lost out to Charles G. Dawes. He resigned when he won the Republican nomination for President in 1928.

The two "almosts":

1. THEODORE ROOSEVELT (1901–09) served as William McKinley's Assistant Secretary of the Navy from 1897 to 1898. He ad-

vocated expansion and war with Spain, and served as acting Secretary during the prolonged absences of ailing Secretary John D. Long. He resigned to volunteer to serve in the Spanish-American War.

2. FRANKLIN DELANO ROOSEVELT (1933–45) served as Woodrow Wilson's Assistant Secretary of the Navy from 1913 to 1920. He proposed expansion of the navy, drew up war contingency plans as early as 1913, and was an early advocate of U.S. entry into World War I. During the war, he directed the mining of waters between Scotland and Norway. He also took two inspection tours of naval bases and war zones in Europe, July–September 1918 and January–February 1919. He resigned in 1920 to accept the Democratic nomination for Vice President under James M. Cox.

65

Presidents Who Won the Nobel Prize

THEODORE ROOSEVELT (1901–09) won the 1906 Nobel Peace Prize for his success in mediating the Treaty of Portsmouth. The treaty ended the Russo-Japanese War of 1904–05, which had been fought over control of Manchuria and Korea. Roosevelt was the first American to win the six-year-old prize. He used the prize money ($36,735) to create a trust fund to promote industrial peace. After the United States entered World War I, he diverted the now-$45,000 trust to aid war victims. His medal is on display in the Roosevelt Room of the White House.

WOODROW WILSON (1913–21) won the 1919 Nobel Peace Prize in recognition of his efforts to achieve world peace and establish the League of Nations. Wilson toured the United States in September 1919, making dozens of speeches in 29 cities in three weeks, urging the United States to participate in the League. He suffered a physical breakdown in Pueblo, Colorado, and returned to Washington, D.C., where he suffered a stroke. The Senate Foreign Relations Committee tried to add reservations to the treaty, which Wilson refused to accept, and so the United States never joined the League of Nations. The League did good work, but ultimately collapsed at the beginning of World War II, and dissolved itself in 1946, making way for the United Nations. His medal is on display at the Woodrow Wilson House in Washington, D.C.

JIMMY CARTER (1977–81) won the 2002 Nobel Peace Prize "for his decades of untiring efforts to find peaceful solutions to international conflicts, to advance democracy and human rights, and to promote economic and social development." The award speech mentioned Carter's efforts to bring about the Camp David Peace Accords between Israel and Egypt in 1978, for which the Nobel Committee actually wanted to give him the prize—along with Menachim Begin and Anwar Sadat—in 1978, but Carter was not nominated in time. His efforts in Haiti in 1994 were also cited, as well as his ongoing campaign for human rights and his work through the Carter Center as election observers in more than 30 elections worldwide. His medal is on display at the Jimmy Carter Library and Museum in Atlanta, Georgia.

66

The First President to Receive More Than 100,000, One Million, 10 Million, and 50 Million Votes

THE FIRST PRESIDENT TO RECEIVE MORE THAN 100,000 POPULAR votes was John Quincy Adams in the election of 1824. Adams received 115,696 popular votes, and 84 electoral votes. His main opponent, Andrew Jackson, won 152,933 popular votes and 99 electoral votes. But since neither candidate had a majority, the election went to the House of Representatives, which chose Adams over Jackson.

The first President to receive more than one million votes was William Henry Harrison in the election of 1840. He got 1,275,017 votes (earning 234 electoral votes) to incumbent President Martin Van Buren's 1,128,702 votes (which translated to 60 electoral votes).

The first President to receive more than 10 million votes was Warren Gamaliel Harding in the election of 1920. Harding's 16,152,200 popular votes was a 77 percent increase over the 9,129,606 votes Woodrow Wilson received in 1916. That increase was due to the adoption of the 19th Amendment, which was ratified in August 1920, and gave women the right to vote.

Harding defeated James M. Cox—who only garnered 9,147,353 popular votes—404 electoral votes to 127.

The first President to receive more than 50 million votes was Ronald Wilson Reagan in the election of 1984. Reagan received 54,281,858 votes on his way to the biggest electoral landslide in U.S. history. Challenger Walter Mondale got 37,457,215 votes, and Reagan won the election with the most electoral votes ever: 525–13.

The only other times a candidate received more than 50 million votes were the elections of 2000 and 2004.

67

The First Losing Presidential Candidate to Receive More Than 100,000, One Million, 10 Million, and 50 Million Votes

THE FIRST LOSING PRESIDENTIAL CANDIDATE TO COLLECT MORE than 100,000 popular votes was Andrew Jackson in the election of 1824. Jackson received 155,872 votes, giving him 99 electoral votes. Victor John Quincy Adams received 105,321 popular votes, and 84 electoral votes, but since neither candidate had a majority (there were two other strong candidates: William H. Crawford, who got 41 electoral votes, and Henry Clay, with 37), the election went to the House of Representatives, which chose Adams. Jackson came back to handily defeat Adams in the election of 1828.

The first losing presidential candidate to receive more than one million popular votes was Martin Van Buren in his bid for re-election in 1840. Van Buren got 1,128,702, which was 48 percent more than he got in his victory in 1836. William Henry Harrison's 1,275,017 votes in victory in 1840 was 132 percent more than he'd gotten in 1836, when he lost with 548,007 votes.

The first losing presidential candidate to receive more than 10 million popular votes was Alfred E. Smith in the election of 1928. He got 15,016,443 votes, losing to Herbert Hoover, who had 21,392,190.

The first losing presidential candidate to receive more than 50 million popular votes was Al Gore in 2000. His 51,003,894 were more than victor George W. Bush's 50,459,211, but Bush won in the electoral college, 271 to 266 (one Gore elector abstained). After Reagan's 1984 victory, Bush and Gore were only the second and third candidates to receive more than 50 million votes. In the election of 2004, Bush became the first to top 60 million votes.

68

Presidential Elections Decided by the House of Representatives

ELECTION OF 1800

Before the adoption of the 12th Amendment, the presidential candidate who received the second-greatest number of electoral votes became the Vice President, and the electors in the electoral college each cast two votes. In the election of 1800, Thomas Jefferson and Aaron Burr each received 73 electoral votes (they each won eight states: Georgia, Kentucky, New York, North Carolina, Pennsylvania, South Carolina, Tennessee, and Virginia). Incumbent John Adams and his vice presidential candidate Charles

Pinckney won seven states (Connecticut, Delaware, Massachusetts, New Hampshire, New Jersey, Rhode Island, and Vermont), garnering 65 electoral votes (Maryland was split).

Though it had been clear during the campaign that Jefferson was the presidential candidate and Burr the vice presidential, Burr refused to concede, and the tie threw the election to the House of Representatives. The House, casting one vote per state (based on the majority of that state's delegation), took 36 ballots between February 11 and 17, 1801. With Alexander Hamilton's help, Jefferson finally prevailed, winning ten states (Georgia, Kentucky, Maryland, New Jersey, New York, North Carolina, Pennsylvania, Tennessee, Vermont, and Virginia) to Burr's four (Connecticut, Massachusetts, New Hampshire, and Rhode Island), with Delaware and South Carolina casting blank ballots. Thus, Jefferson was declared President and Burr Vice President. This deadlock was the reason the 12th Amendment was proposed and adopted.

ELECTION OF 1824

This was the last election before strong political parties took control, and the four strong candidates running for President were all considered Democrat-Republicans. The outcome turned on sectional rivalries and personalities.

Andrew Jackson received 155,872 popular votes, winning 11 states (Alabama, Illinois, Indiana, Louisiana, Maryland, Mississippi, New Jersey, North Carolina, Pennsylvania, South Carolina, and Tennessee) and 99 electoral votes. John Quincy Adams received 105,321 popular votes, winning seven states (Connecticut, Maine, Massachusetts, New Hampshire, New York, Rhode Island, and Vermont) and 84 electoral votes. Henry Clay received 46,587 popular votes, winning three states (Kentucky, Missouri, and Ohio) and 37 electoral votes. William H. Crawford received 44,282 popular votes, winning three states (Delaware, Georgia, and Virginia) and 41 electoral votes.

None of the candidates had a majority of electoral votes, so in accordance with the 12th Amendment, the election went to the House of Representatives, which had to choose from among the top-three electoral vote-getters, which dropped Clay from consideration. Clay supported Adams, and on February 9, 1825, the House voted by state, electing Adams on the first ballot. He won 13 states (Connecticut, Illinois, Kentucky, Louisiana, Maine, Maryland, Massachusetts, Missouri, New Hampshire, New York, Ohio, Rhode Island, and Vermont); Jackson won seven (Alabama, Indiana, Mississippi, New Jersey, Pennsylvania, South Carolina, and Tennessee); and Crawford won four (Delaware, Georgia, North Carolina, and Virginia).

John C. Calhoun received 182 electoral votes for Vice President, easily winning over five other candidates (including future Presidents Andrew Jackson and Martin Van Buren), who split 79.

Clay ran again for President in 1832 (losing to Andrew Jackson, 219 to 49 electoral votes) and again in 1844 (losing to James Knox Polk, 170 to 105).

ELECTION OF 1876
During the ballot counting, while it looked like Democrat Samuel Tilden was winning (indeed, Republican Rutherford Hayes told a reporter he thought he had lost), the returns from Florida, Louisiana, and South Carolina (as well as one electoral vote from Oregon) were disputed. The electoral vote (excluding the disputed votes) was 184–166 for Tilden, one vote short of the majority needed for election.

To resolve the dispute, Congress established a 15-man commission, comprised of five senators (three Republicans and two Democrats), five representatives (two Republicans and three Democrats), and five Supreme Court justices (two appointed by Republicans, two appointed by Democrats, and one chosen by the other four). The commission voted along strict party lines, 8–7, in

February 1877 to award the 21 disputed votes to Hayes. Congress ratified the decision in joint session on March 2, declaring Hayes the winner and William Wheeler the Vice President.

The final vote totals were 4,284,757 votes for Tilden (184 electoral votes), 4,033,950 votes for Hayes (185 electoral votes).

NOT QUITE: THE ELECTION OF 1836

Martin Van Buren won 51 percent of the popular vote, enough to win 170 electoral votes (and the election), beating William Henry Harrison (73 electoral votes), Hugh Lawson White (26), Daniel Webster (14), and undeclared candidate Willie P. Mangum (11). The electors from Virginia, however, were unwilling to vote for Van Buren's running mate, Richard M. Johnson of Kentucky. Instead, they voted for William Smith of Alabama. Thus, Johnson did not receive a majority of electoral votes, and for the only time, the vice presidential election was thrown to the Senate to decide. In February 1837, the Senate elected Johnson over Francis Granger of New York, 33 to 16.

69

Most Popular Colleges Attended by the Presidents

THE MOST POPULAR COLLEGES PRESIDENTS-TO-BE GRADUATED FROM:

1. Harvard. Five Presidents graduated from Harvard, one from Harvard Law, and one more from Harvard Business School: JOHN ADAMS (graduated in 1755), JOHN QUINCY ADAMS (1787),

THEODORE ROOSEVELT (1880), FRANKLIN DELANO ROOSEVELT (1904), and JOHN KENNEDY (1940). RUTHERFORD B. HAYES graduated from the law school in 1845, and GEORGE W. BUSH received his MBA from the business school in 1975.

2. Yale. Three Presidents graduated from Yale's undergraduate school, and two more from Yale Law School. WILLIAM HOWARD TAFT (graduated in 1878), GEORGE H.W. BUSH (1948), and GEORGE W. BUSH (1968) were undergraduates. The two law school graduates were GERALD FORD (1941) and BILL CLINTON (1973).

Only three other colleges can claim more than one future President:

3. The College of William and Mary. THOMAS JEFFERSON attended from 1760 to 1762, and though he did not receive a degree, he completed his studies. JAMES MONROE also studied at William and Mary, but dropped out to fight in the Revolutionary War. JOHN TYLER actually graduated from the school, in 1807.

4 (tie). The College of New Jersey. JAMES MADISON graduated in 1771, and WOODROW WILSON in 1879. Later, the school was renamed Princeton University.

4 (tie). The U.S. Military Academy at West Point. ULYSSES GRANT graduated 21st in his class of 39 in 1843. DWIGHT EISENHOWER graduated 61st of 164 in 1915.

The other colleges that can claim one President each are: the University of North Carolina (Polk); Bowdoin College of Maine (Pierce); Dickinson College of Pennsylvania (Buchanan); Kenyon College of Ohio (Hayes, undergraduate); Williams College of Massachusetts (Garfield); Union College of New York

(Arthur); Miami University of Ohio (BHarrison); University of Cincinnati Law School (Taft, graduate); Johns Hopkins (Wilson, Ph.D.); Ohio Central College (Harding); Amherst College of Massachusetts (Coolidge); Stanford University (Hoover); Southwest Texas State Teachers College (LBJohnson); Whittier College of California (Nixon, undergraduate); Duke Law School (Nixon, graduate); University of Michigan (Ford, undergraduate); the U.S. Naval Academy, Annapolis (Carter); Eureka College of Illinois (Reagan); and Georgetown University (Clinton, undergraduate).

70

The Presidents Who Did Not Attend College or Did Not Receive Degrees

FOUR PRESIDENTS HAD REMARKABLY LITTLE FORMAL EDUCATION:

1. GEORGE WASHINGTON had almost no formal education and did not attend college (of the Founding Fathers, he was unique in not knowing French, which was the language of diplomacy).

2. ZACHARY TAYLOR's education was very basic, and he did not attend college.

3. ABRAHAM LINCOLN had no college degree. He estimated that he had about one year of formal education.

4. ANDREW JOHNSON had absolutely no formal education. He taught himself to read as an adult.

Three Presidents attended colleges, but did not graduate:

1. JAMES MONROE was a student at the College of William and Mary, but dropped out to fight in the Revolutionary War. He later studied law under THOMAS JEFFERSON.

2. WILLIAM HENRY HARRISON, early in life, thought he was destined for a career in medicine. He attended three different colleges, but didn't receive a degree from any of them.

3. WILLIAM McKINLEY entered Allegheny College as a 17-year-old junior, but illness forced him to withdraw within the year. Following the Civil War, he attended Albany (New York) Law School in 1866 and 1867, but dropped out before graduation. He was admitted to the Ohio bar in March 1867.

Several Presidents studied law under other lawyers before being admitted to the bar. This was mostly in the time before law schools. Nevertheless, they had no college degrees:

1. ANDREW JACKSON left the Waxhaw region of the North Carolina–South Carolina border in 1784 for Salisbury, North Carolina. There, he studied law for two and a half years under the tutelage of lawyers Spruce McCay and John Stokes, and was admitted to the North Carolina bar in 1787.

2. MARTIN VAN BUREN began studying law under local lawyer Francis Sylvester at the age of 14 in his native Kinderhook, New York. He worked for Sylvester for six years (summing up a routine case before a jury at age 15). He moved to New York City for another year of apprenticeship, to William P. Van Ness, and then was admitted to the New York bar in 1803.

3. MILLARD FILLMORE worked for and studied under county judge Walter Wood in Montville, New York, for two years. He left in

1821, following a dispute with the judge, and returned home. The following year, he continued his studies under Asa Rice and Joseph Clary, and then was admitted to the New York bar in 1823.

4. GROVER CLEVELAND left home in upstate New York for Cleveland, Ohio, in 1855, but stopped in Buffalo to visit his uncle and wound up settling there. Cleveland studied law at the Buffalo office of Rogers, Bowen, and Rogers, and was admitted to the New York bar in 1859.

71

The Five States That Voted Most Often for the Winning Presidential Candidate

THERE HAVE BEEN 55 PRESIDENTIAL ELECTIONS SINCE THE ADOPTION OF the Constitution. The first was in 1789, when George Washington was unanimously elected by the electoral college. Some states have voted in all 55, others (which joined the Union later) voted in fewer elections, down to Hawaii, which joined in 1959 and has voted in 12 elections. Therefore, this list is based on "winning percentage": the states that voted for the winning candidate the greatest percent of the time they have voted in a presidential election. (The states that seceded during the Civil War missed one or two elections, depending on when they were readmitted to the Union.)

1. New Mexico. Since becoming a state on January 6, 1912, New Mexico has voted for the winning candidate in 22 of the 24 elections in which it participated, or 91.67 percent.

2. Illinois. The 21st state, became a state on December 3, 1818. Its people have voted for the winning presidential candidate 39 times of the 48 elections in which they participated. In addition, in 1824, the people voted for ANDREW JACKSON, who lost the election (even though he'd won a plurality of the electoral votes). Instead, the election was thrown to the House of Representatives, and voting by state, Illinois voted for the winner, JOHN QUINCY ADAMS. This gives Illinois a percentage of 85.11. (If 1824 is counted as a loser, the state drops to 82.98 percent, which would rank it fourth.)

3. Idaho. On July 3, 1890, Idaho became the 43rd state. Since then, the people of Idaho have voted for the winning presidential candidate 22 times, and chosen the losing candidate only four times: 84.62 percent.

4. Ohio. Ohio became the 17th state when its residents adopted the Constitution on March 1, 1803. Ohioans have voted for the winning presidential candidate 42 times, the losing candidate eight times, and both a loser and the winner in 1824. In the election of 1824, the people of Ohio voted for Henry Clay, who came in fourth in the electoral college voting. The election (in line with the dictates of the 12th Amendment) was thrown to the House of Representatives to decide from among the top three vote-getters. This meant Ohio's candidate, Clay, was out of the running, and the Ohio delegation voted for the eventual winner, JOHN QUINCY ADAMS. With a record of 43 victories out of 51 elections, Ohio's percentage is 84.31. (If 1824 is counted as a loser, the state drops to 82.35 percent, which would rank it fifth.)

5. Arizona. Since becoming the 48th state on February 14, 1912, Arizona has voted for the winning candidate in 20 of the 24 elections in which it participated, or 83.33 percent.

The first state on this list to have voted in all 55 elections is Pennsylvania, with a record of supporting the victor 44 times (80 percent), which ranks it ninth.

72

The Five States That Voted Least Often for the Winning Presidential Candidate

THIS LIST IS BASED ON THE "LOSING PERCENTAGE" OF ELECTIONS: states that voted for the winning candidate the least, in terms of percentage, when participating in presidential elections. (The states that seceded during the Civil War missed one or two elections, depending on when they were readmitted to the Union.)

1. Alabama. Since becoming the 22nd state on December 14, 1819, Alabama has participated in 46 elections (the state did not vote in the election of 1864, during its secession to the Confederacy). In those 46 elections, Alabama voted for the winning presidential candidate 24 times, for a winning percentage of only 52.17.

2. Mississippi. Since becoming the 20th state on December 10, 1817, Mississippi has participated in 45 elections (the state did not vote in the elections of 1864 or 1868, during its secession to the Confederacy). In those 45 elections, Mississippi voted for the winning presidential candidate 24 times, for a winning percentage of only 53.33.

3. Texas. Texas was the only independent nation to join the United States as a state, when it signed the Constitution on December 29, 1845, making it the 28th state. In the ensuing 40 elections, the people of Texas voted for the winning candidate 23 times, amassing a winning percentage of 57.50.

4. South Carolina. The only one of the original 13 states to appear on either this list or its complement (states that have voted for the winning candidate most often), South Carolina missed the election of 1864 (when it seceded to the Confederacy during the Civil War). In the other 54 elections, South Carolina racked up a record of 32 victories, for 59.26 percent. In the election of 1800 the people of South Carolina voted for Thomas Jefferson, the eventual winner, but because Jefferson and Aaron Burr were tied in the electoral college, the House of Representatives was forced to choose the winner. Voting in the House, South Carolina cast a blank ballot.

5. Arkansas. Since becoming the 25th state on June 15, 1836, the people of Arkansas have voted for President 42 times (they skipped the election of 1864, when the state had seceded during the Civil War). Arkansas voted for the winning candidate 25 times, for a percentage of 59.52.

Following ratification of the 23rd Amendment in 1961, the District of Columbia was granted a vote in presidential elections. In the 11 elections in which D.C. has participated, it has voted for the winner only four times, giving it a percentage of 36.36.

The first state on this list to have voted in all 55 elections is Delaware, with a record of supporting the victor 34 times (61.82 percent), which ranks it seventh on this not-voting-for-the-winner list.

73

Elections in Which No Candidates Had Previously Been President or Vice President

THREE-QUARTERS OF THE QUADRENNIAL ELECTIONS HAVE BOASTED at least one major party candidate who was currently or had previously been President or Vice President. The election of 2008 is shaping up to be one of the minority. There are only six eligible Presidents and Vice Presidents: Vice President Dick Cheney (probably won't run due to health reasons), former Vice President Al Gore (lost the election of 2000), former President George H.W. Bush (lost his bid for reelection in 1992, he'll be 84 in 2008), former Vice President Dan Quayle, former President Jimmy Carter (lost his bid for reelection in 1980, he'll be 84 in 2008), and former Vice President Walter Mondale (lost the election of 1984, he'll be 80 in 2008).

In every election there have been more than two candidates, but the few times the third-party candidates were former Presidents or Vice Presidents, they were running against incumbents, so those elections do not appear on this list.

1952: The election of 1952 was the last to see no Presidents or Vice Presidents on the major party tickets. Republican General DWIGHT D. EISENHOWER and Senator RICHARD M.

NIXON defeated Democrat Adlai E. Stevenson and John J. Sparkman.

1920: The election of 1920 had no Presidents or Vice Presidents running, but three of the four major candidates would later serve as President. Republican WARREN G. HARDING won the election with vice presidential candidate CALVIN COOLIDGE, who would succeed upon Harding's death in 1923. Democrat James M. Cox headed the losing ticket with vice presidential candidate FRANKLIN D. ROOSEVELT, who would later win four elections as President (1932, 1936, 1940, and 1944).

1908: The election of 1908 saw Republicans WILLIAM HOWARD TAFT and James Sherman defeat Democrats William Jennings Bryan and John Kern. This was Bryan's third losing run for the presidency (after 1896 and 1900).

1896: In the election of 1896, Republican WILLIAM McKINLEY was elected with Garret Hobart as his number two, defeating William Jennings Bryan (in his first run for the presidency) and Arthur Sewall.

1884: The election of 1884—the first of three in which Democrat GROVER CLEVELAND would run (winning, losing, and then winning)—saw Cleveland and Thomas Hendricks (who had run in 1876) defeat Republicans James Blaine and John Logan.

1880: The election of 1880 was the second of three in a row with inexperienced candidates. Republicans JAMES A. GARFIELD and CHESTER A. ARTHUR defeated Democrats Winfield Hancock and William English.

1876: The election of 1876 saw Republicans RUTHERFORD B. HAYES and William A. Wheeler defeat Democrats Samuel J. Tilden and Thomas Hendricks (who would win the vice presidency eight years later).

1868: In the election of 1868, Republicans Ulysses S. Grant and Schuyler Colfax defeated Democrats Horatio Seymour and Francis Blair.

1852: The election of 1852 saw Democrat Franklin Pierce and William R. King defeat Whig Winfield Scott and William Alexander Graham.

1844: The election of 1844 saw Democrat James Knox Polk and George M. Dallas defeat Whig Henry Clay and Theodore Frelinghuysen. Though Clay had never been President or Vice President, this was his third election as a presidential candidate (following 1824 and 1832).

1824: The election of 1824 was more of an electoral free-for-all. In the last election before political parties started to exert major influence, all four major candidates were Democrat-Republicans, and none received a majority of the electoral votes, so the House of Representatives chose the victor. The four candidates who received electoral votes were: eventual victor John Quincy Adams (84 electoral votes), Andrew Jackson (99), Henry Clay (37), and William Harris Crawford (41). The candidates who received electoral votes for Vice President were John C. Calhoun (182), Nathan Sanford (30), Nathaniel Macon (24), Andrew Jackson (13), Martin Van Buren (nine), and Henry Clay (two).

1816: The election of 1816 saw Democrat-Republicans James Monroe and Daniel D. Tompkins defeat Federalist Rufus King and his running mates (who varied from state to state): Robert Goodloe Harper, John Eager Howard, John Marshall, and James Ross.

1808: The election of 1808 saw Democrat-Republicans James Madison and George Clinton defeat Federalists Charles Pinckney and Rufus King.

1789: The election of 1789, of course, couldn't have any experienced candidates, since it chose the first President. GEORGE WASHINGTON was unanimously elected, with JOHN ADAMS elected Vice President.

74

Presidents Who Never Held Elective Office Before Being Elected President

1. ZACHARY TAYLOR (1849–50). After long military service, General Taylor was nominated in 1848 as a war hero, having just defeated Santa Anna at Buena Vista in the Mexican War. He previously fought in the War of 1812, the Black Hawk War (1832), and the second Seminole War (1837).

2. ULYSSES S. GRANT (1869–77). He graduated from West Point in 1843, fought in the Mexican War (1846–48), and then resigned from the army in 1854. He was named colonel and then brigadier general of the Illinois Volunteers during the Civil War, and then President Lincoln placed him in command of all Union armies. When President Johnson suspended Secretary of War Stanton (leading to his impeachment), he appointed Grant Secretary of War, but Grant was never confirmed in that post.

3. HERBERT HOOVER (1929–33). While serving as chief engineer of imperial mines in China, he directed food relief for victims of the Boxer Rebellion. He later directed the American Relief Committee, London (1914–15), and the U.S. Commission for Relief

in Belgium (1915–19). He was U.S. Food Administrator (1917–19), American Relief Administrator (1918–23), and in charge of Russian Relief (1918–23), before becoming Secretary of Commerce (1923–28).

4. Dwight D. Eisenhower (1953–61). He graduated from West Point in 1915, and later served on General Douglas MacArthur's staff in the Philippines (1935–39). In 1943, he was promoted to four-star general, and later appointed Supreme Allied Commander in Europe. He got his fifth star at the end of 1944. In 1948, he became president of Columbia University, and in 1950, Commander of NATO forces.

FOUR

ON THE JOB

The Five Oldest Presidents

CONSIDERED BY AGE AT INAUGURATION, THE LIST RUNS AS FOLLOWS:

1. RONALD REAGAN was 17 days shy of his 70th birthday when he was inaugurated on January 20, 1989, and 17 days shy of his 78th birthday when he retired eight years later. To best his record, the President who wins the election of 2008 will have to have been born before February 6, 1938.

2. WILLIAM HENRY HARRISON was 68 years, 23 days old when he was inaugurated on March 4, 1841. The President who served the shortest term (31 days), he was the first to die in office, so he was only 68 years, 54 days old when he left office. He was also the oldest for 140 years, until Reagan came along.

3. JAMES BUCHANAN was 65 years, 315 days old when he was inaugurated in 1857, and 69 years, 315 days old when he retired from office.

4. GEORGE H.W. BUSH was 64 years, 222 days old—a relative youngster—when he succeeded the oldest President, Reagan, in 1989, and 68 years, 222 days old when he left office.

5. ZACHARY TAYLOR was 64 years, 100 days old when he was inaugurated in 1849. The second President to die in office, he was

65 years, 227 days old at his death. He was the second-oldest President until JAMES BUCHANAN was elected. To knock him off the list, the President elected in 2008 will have to have been born before October 12, 1945.

Considering age at the time the President left office, Dwight David Eisenhower moves into second place. He was only 62 years, 98 days old when he was inaugurated in 1953, putting him sixth on the list, but serving two full terms (he and Reagan are the only two on this list to have served eight years as President), he was 70 years, 98 days old when he retired. And, of course, Buchanan and Bush would move ahead of Harrison if the list were "age at the time the President left office."

76

The Five Youngest Presidents

ARTICLE II, SECTION 1 OF THE CONSTITUTION REQUIRES A PRESIDENT to be at least 35 years old.

1. THEODORE ROOSEVELT. Born on October 27, 1858, he was 42 years, 322 days old when he was inaugurated on September 14, 1901, after WILLIAM McKINLEY was assassinated. To beat Roosevelt's record as the youngest President in the election of 2008, the newly elected President will have to have been born after March 4, 1966.

2. JOHN F. KENNEDY. Born on May 29, 1917, he was 43 years, 236 days old when he took the oath of office on January 20, 1961,

after winning the election of 1960. To beat Kennedy's record as the youngest President elected, the winner of the election of 2008 will have to have been born after May 29, 1965.

3. BILL CLINTON. Born on August 19, 1946, he was 46 years, 154 days old when he was inaugurated on January 20, 1993.

4. ULYSSES S. GRANT. Born on April 27, 1822, he was 46 years, 311 days old when he was inaugurated on March 4, 1869.

5. GROVER CLEVELAND. Born on March 18, 1837, he was 14 days shy of his 48th birthday when he was inaugurated on March 4, 1885.

In order to join this list (and knock Cleveland off), the President who wins the election of 2008 will have to have been born after January 6, 1961.

77

Presidents Who Won Election by the Largest Margins

POPULAR VOTE TOTALS FOR THE ELECTIONS PRIOR TO 1824 ARE either unreliable or unavailable, so for the first few elections, we can only consider electoral votes. Starting with 1824, we have popular vote totals, of varying degrees of exactitude. And it's frequently difficult, if not impossible, to get exact numbers, because there are almost always votes for unknowns, votes for candidates on the ballot in only a few of the states, and write-in votes. Therefore, this list is presented as two lists: electoral vote margins, which are precise, and popular vote margins, which are approximate.

Largest Electoral Vote Margins

It's almost questionable whether to include George Washington on this list, since he was unopposed when he was first chosen President.

1 (tie). GEORGE WASHINGTON in the election of 1792 received all 132 electoral votes cast, giving him 100 percent of the electoral vote.

1 (tie). GEORGE WASHINGTON in the election of 1789 received all 69 electoral votes cast, giving him 100 percent of the electoral vote.

3. JAMES MONROE in the election of 1820 received 231 of the 232 electoral votes cast, giving him 99.57 percent of the electoral vote. Monroe was unopposed in his bid for reelection, but one elector from New Hampshire cast his ballot for JOHN QUINCY ADAMS. According to legend, it was to maintain Washington's record as the only unanimously elected President, but other indications point to the fact that the elector, Governor William Plumer, did not like Monroe, and voted against him in earnest.

4. FRANKLIN DELANO ROOSEVELT in the election of 1936 received 523 of the 531 electoral votes cast, giving him 98.49 percent of the electoral vote. This was Roosevelt's first reelection, after coming to office during the Great Depression and bringing hope with his New Deal program. Republican Alf Landon won only Maine and Vermont.

5. RONALD REAGAN in the election of 1984 received 525 of the 538 electoral votes cast, giving him 97.58 percent of the electoral

vote. Reagan's reelection was almost a coronation, with his popularity flying and his opponent, former Vice President Walter Mondale, struggling. Mondale won the electoral votes of only his home state, Minnesota, and the District of Columbia.

6. RICHARD NIXON in the election of 1972 received 520 of the 538 electoral votes cast, giving him 96.65 percent of the electoral vote. Nixon's opponent, Democrat George McGovern of South Dakota, received only the electoral votes of Massachusetts and the District of Columbia. Libertarian John Hospers of California received one electoral vote from Virginia.

7. THOMAS JEFFERSON in the election of 1804 received 162 of the 176 electoral votes cast, giving him 92.05 percent of the electoral vote. After the confusion of the election of 1800, Jefferson prevailed over the dying Federalist Party, winning all but two states—Connecticut and Delaware—over South Carolina's Charles Cotesworth Pinckney.

Largest Popular Vote Margins

Only four presidential candidates have won more than 60 percent of the popular vote.

1. FRANKLIN DELANO ROOSEVELT in the election of 1936. Roosevelt was first elected in 1932 during the Great Depression, and though his policies hadn't solved the country's ills, he came into office with sweeping changes and programs, and the country felt invigorated, overwhelmingly returning him to a second term in office. He received 27,751,597 popular votes, about 62.5 percent of the total cast. His opponents came closer when he broke with tradition to run for a third and fourth term, but he still won 55 and 53.8 percent of the popular votes cast in those elections (in 1932 he got 59.1 percent of the popular vote).

2. RICHARD NIXON in the election of 1972. He would later resign because of the Watergate scandal, which involved actions during the campaign, but meanwhile won reelection easily, garnering 47,165,234 popular votes, which was 61.8 percent of the total.

3. WARREN G. HARDING in the election of 1920. The first election in which women had the vote was also Socialist Eugene V. Debs's fourth election on the national stage (he won no electoral votes, but got 3.5 percent of the popular vote). Harding's 16,152,200 popular votes was 61.6 percent of the total, easily defeating Democrat James Cox (and his vice presidential candidate, FRANKLIN DELANO ROOSEVELT, who made quite a comeback in 1932).

4. LYNDON BAINES JOHNSON in the election of 1964. Succeeding the immensely popular President Kennedy upon the latter's assassination in 1963, Johnson continued most of his policies and was pretty much a shoo-in over Republican Barry Goldwater. Johnson got 43,126,506 popular votes, which was 61.3 percent of the total.

5. RONALD REAGAN in the election of 1984. Democrat Walter Mondale seemed to struggle from the time he won the nomination all the way through election day. Reagan got 54,281,858 popular votes, 59.2 percent of the total. This translated into a 97.6 to 2.4 percent electoral vote count, an incredible landslide.

78

Presidents Who Won Election
by the Smallest Margins

POPULAR VOTE TOTALS FOR THE ELECTIONS PRIOR TO 1824 ARE either unreliable or unavailable, so for the first few elections, we can only consider electoral votes. Starting with 1824, we have popular vote totals, of varying degrees of exactitude. And it's frequently difficult, if not impossible, to get exact numbers, because there are almost always votes for unknowns, votes for candidates on the ballot in only a few of the states, and write-in votes. Therefore, this list is presented as two lists: electoral vote margins, which are precise, and popular vote margins, which are approximate.

Smallest Electoral Vote Margins

1. JOHN QUINCY ADAMS, in the election of 1824, received only 32.18 percent of the electoral votes (84 of the 261 votes cast), but because none of the four candidates had a majority (Andrew Jackson's 99 electoral votes were only 37.93 percent), the election was thrown to the House of Representatives. Voting by state, the House gave the election to Adams. He is the only President to have lost both the popular and electoral votes yet still won the presidency.

2. THOMAS JEFFERSON, in the election of 1800, received 73 of the 146 electoral votes, which was precisely 50 percent. Unfortunately, Aaron Burr, who was assumed to be running as Jefferson's Vice President, received as many electoral votes (this, during the time when the candidate receiving the second-greatest number of electoral votes became Vice President). After much maneuvering in the House of Representatives, Jefferson was named President and Burr Vice President. It was this election that prompted the adoption of the 12th Amendment, making presidential and vice presidential candidates run as a ticket. Jefferson's reelection four years later was much different: He won 92.05 percent of the electoral votes.

3. RUTHERFORD B. HAYES in the election of 1876. Soon after election day, Hayes assumed he'd lost, and said so in public. His opponent, Samuel J. Tilden, won the popular vote, and was leading in electoral votes, 184 to 166 (185 would have been a majority). The returns from Florida, Louisiana, and South Carolina were disputed, and Congress appointed a 15-man committee to judge the issue. In February 1877, the committee voted 8–7, along party lines, to award all the disputed votes to Hayes, giving him 185 electoral votes (50.14 percent) and the election.

4. GEORGE W. BUSH in the election of 2000. There were questions and legal challenges over the popular vote counts in Florida. Eventually, the matter was brought to the Supreme Court, which voted 5–4 to stop the recounting at a point when Bush was in the lead, giving him Florida's electoral votes, and a total of 271 electoral votes (50.37 percent). Vice President Al Gore received 266 votes (one elector from Washington, D.C., abstained). In his reelection four years later, Bush fared slightly better, garnering 53.16 percent of the electoral votes.

5. JOHN ADAMS in the election of 1796. The first contested presidential election in the United States was the closest to not require

some other form of intervention. John Adams won nine states and Thomas Jefferson won seven. The electoral votes were 68 for Jefferson, and 71 (51.08 percent) for Adams. Jefferson, as the runner-up, became Vice President, setting the stage for his even closer election four years later (see above).

Smallest Popular Vote Margins

More than a quarter of all Presidents were elected with fewer than half the popular votes cast. Ignoring the statistically small numbers of votes for unknowns, votes for candidates on the ballot in one or only a few states, and write-in votes, the candidates chosen by the smallest percentage of voters are:

1. John Quincy Adams in the election of 1824. The first election with accurate popular vote totals was a wide-open contest. Andrew Jackson's 155,872 popular votes was 44.3 percent of the total and garnered 99 electoral votes. John Quincy Adams's 105,321 popular votes was only 29.9 percent of the total, but with two other strong contenders (Henry Clay and William H. Crawford), no candidate was able to win a majority of the electoral votes, and the House of Representatives, following the dictates of the 12th Amendment, elected Adams.

It should also be noted that six states (Delaware, Georgia, Louisiana, New York, South Carolina, and Vermont) did not have popular votes in 1824. Their state legislatures chose their electors.

2. Abraham Lincoln, in the election of 1860, won 1,866,352 votes for 39.9 percent of the total. The new Republican party was united behind him, but the Democratic Party was split between northern (Stephen A. Douglas) and southern (John C. Breckenridge) factions, and the remains of the Whig Party, which refused

to join the Republicans, supporting John Bell. Thus, a four-way race gave Lincoln the election with 59.41 percent of the electoral vote (180 electoral votes), but less than 40 percent of the popular vote. Douglas's 1,375,157 votes were only 29.4 percent of the total cast, while Breckenridge got 845,763 (18.1 percent) and Bell, 589,581 (12.6 percent).

3. WOODROW WILSON in the election of 1912. Wilson's victory, in which he won only 6,286,214 votes (42.2 percent of the total), was due to former President THEODORE ROOSEVELT running on a third-party ticket. It was, however, broad-based support, and won Wilson 435 electoral votes (81.92 percent of the total). Roosevelt was the President who came closest to winning a third term before his cousin Franklin managed it in 1940. After four years of retirement, Roosevelt had come back to challenge his handpicked successor, WILLIAM HOWARD TAFT, and pulled 4,216,020 votes (28.3 percent of the total), beating Taft's 3,483,922 (23.4 percent). Socialist Eugene V. Debs, in his third campaign, garnered 901,255 votes (6.1 percent).

4. BILL CLINTON in 1992. His 44,908,254 votes were good for only 43.3 percent of the total, but it did give him 370 electoral votes (68.77 percent). He beat sitting President GEORGE H.W. BUSH's 39,102,343 votes (37.7 percent), while independent candidate Ross Perot pulled in 19,741,065 votes (19 percent) in his first of two runs for the presidency.

5. RICHARD NIXON in 1968. He lost to JOHN KENNEDY in 1960, while he was the sitting Vice President, and swore off politics quite publicly in 1962, but his comeback in 1968 won Nixon the presidency in a squeaker. He got 31,785,480 votes, which was only 43.6 percent. Fortunately for Nixon, he was in a three-man race. Vice President Hubert Humphrey polled 31,275,166 votes (42.9 per-

cent) while breakaway Democrat George Wallace, running under the American Independent banner, got 9,906,473 votes (13.6 percent). The close popular vote race was also close electorally, with Nixon winning 301 electoral votes for 55.95 percent and victory.

In addition to the above five, eight other candidates were elected with less than 50 percent of the popular votes. In chronological order, they are:

1. JAMES POLK in the election of 1844: Polk, 1,337,243 (49.6 percent); Henry Clay, 1,299,068 (48.1 percent); James G. Birney, 62,300 (two percent).

2. ZACHARY TAYLOR in the election of 1848: Taylor, 1,360,101 (47.4 percent); Lewis Cass, 1,220,544 (42.5 percent); Martin Van Buren, 291,501 (10.1 percent).

3. JAMES BUCHANAN in the election of 1856: Buchanan, 1,927,995 (46 percent); John C. Frémont, 1,391,555 (33.2 percent); Millard Fillmore, 873,053 (20.8 percent).

4. RUTHERFORD B. HAYES in the election of 1876: Hayes, 4,033,950 (48.5 percent); Samuel J. Tilden, 4,284,757 (51.5 percent). See above.

5. BENJAMIN HARRISON in the election of 1888: Harrison, 5,444,337 (49.6 percent); Grover Cleveland, 5,540,050 (50.4 percent).

6. GROVER CLEVELAND in the election of 1892: Cleveland, 5,554,414 (47.2 percent); Benjamin Harrison, 5,190,802 (44.1 percent); James B. Weaver, 1,027,329 (8.7 percent).

7. HARRY S TRUMAN in the election of 1948: Truman, 24,105,812 (49.8 percent); Thomas E. Dewey, 21,970,065 (45.4 percent);

Strom Thurmond, 1,169,021 (2.4 percent); Henry A. Wallace, 1,157,172 (2.4 percent).

8. GEORGE W. BUSH in the election of 2000: Bush, 50,459,211 (48.4 percent); Al Gore, 51,003,894 (48.9 percent); Ralph Nader, 2,834,410 (2.7 percent).

79

The Five Presidents Who Were the Greatest Number of Years Older Than Their Predecessors

1. RONALD WILSON REAGAN was 13 years, 237 days older than JIMMY CARTER. Reagan was born February 6, 1911, and served 1981–89. Carter was born October 1, 1924, and served 1977–81. Reagan was older than four of his five immediate predecessors: Carter, Ford (born July 14, 1913, served 1974–77), Nixon (born January 9, 1913, served 1969–74), and Kennedy (born May 29, 1917, served 1961–63).

2. JAMES BUCHANAN was 13 years, 214 days older than FRANKLIN PIERCE. Buchanan was born April 23, 1791, and served 1857–61. Pierce was born November 23, 1804, and served 1853–57.

3. ZACHARY TAYLOR was ten years, 343 days older than JAMES KNOX POLK. Taylor was born November 24, 1784, and served 1849–50. Polk was born November 2, 1795, and served 1845–49.

4. WILLIAM HENRY HARRISON was nine years, 299 days older than MARTIN VAN BUREN. Harrison was born February 9, 1773, and

served March 4–April 4, 1841. Van Buren was born December 5, 1782, and served 1837–41.

5. LYNDON BAINES JOHNSON was eight years, 275 days older than JOHN FITZGERALD KENNEDY. Johnson was born August 27, 1908, and served 1963–69 (succeeding to office upon Kennedy's death). Kennedy was born May 29, 1917, and served 1961–63.

Ten other Presidents were older than their predecessors, anywhere from 44 days to four and a half years.

80

The Five Presidents Who Were the Greatest Number of Years Younger Than Their Predecessors

1. JOHN FITZGERALD KENNEDY was 26 years, 227 days younger than DWIGHT DAVID EISENHOWER. Kennedy was born May 29, 1917, and served 1961–63. Eisenhower was born October 14, 1890, and served 1953–61.

2. BILL CLINTON is 22 years, 68 days younger than GEORGE H.W. BUSH. Clinton was born August 19, 1946, and served 1993–2001. Bush was born June 12, 1924, and served 1989–93.

3. ABRAHAM LINCOLN was 17 years, 295 days younger than JAMES BUCHANAN. Lincoln was born February 12, 1809, and served 1861–65. Buchanan was born April 23, 1791, and served

1857–61. Lincoln was only four years, 81 days younger than Buchanan's predecessor, FRANKLIN PIERCE.

4. JOHN TYLER was 17 years, 48 days younger than WILLIAM HENRY HARRISON. Tyler was born March 29, 1790, and served 1841–45 (succeeding to office upon Harrison's death). Harrison was born February 9, 1773, and served March 4–April 4, 1841. Tyler was only seven years, 114 days younger than Harrison's predecessor, MARTIN VAN BUREN.

5. THEODORE ROOSEVELT was 15 years, 271 days younger than WILLIAM MCKINLEY. Roosevelt was born October 27, 1858, and served 1901–09 (succeeding to office upon McKinley's death). McKinley was born January 29, 1843, and served 1897–1901.

Martin Van Buren just misses the list by six days. He was 15 years, 265 days younger than Andrew Jackson. Van Buren was born December 5, 1782, and served 1837–41. Jackson was born March 15, 1767, and served 1829–37.

81

Presidents Who Served Two Full Terms

OF THE 42 PEOPLE TO SERVE AS PRESIDENT, 11 HAVE SERVED TWO complete, four-year terms, nine of them as one eight-year block each: Thomas Jefferson (1801–09), James Madison (1809–17), James Monroe (1817–25), Andrew Jackson (1829–37), Ulysses S. Grant (1869–77), Woodrow Wilson (1913–21), Dwight Eisenhower (1953–61), Ronald Reagan (1981–89), and Bill Clinton (1993–2001). Through Wilson's term, inauguration day was March 4 (which was also the day they left office). From Eisenhower on, inauguration day was January 20.

Franklin Delano Roosevelt served two complete, consecutive, four-year terms, but then went on to be elected to a third and a fourth term. Dying months after being inaugurated for the fourth time, he served 12 years and one month, from March 4, 1933 to April 12, 1945. Inauguration day was moved from March 4 to January 20 during Roosevelt's first term, so he was inaugurated on March 4, 1933, January 20, 1937, January 20, 1941, and January 20, 1945.

Grover Cleveland is the only President to serve two nonconsecutive terms. He was first elected in 1884, then defeated in his bid for reelection in 1888 by Benjamin Harrison. Cleveland came back in 1892 to beat Harrison. His two complete, nonconsecutive, four-year terms were from 1885 to 1889, and then from 1893 to 1897.

George Washington is not on this list because his first term wasn't four years long. The election of the first President came in early 1789, soon after the Constitution was ratified. By the time Washington and first Vice President John Adams were notified of their election, and reported to New York City (then the capital), it was well into April. In fact, Adams arrived before Washington, and was inaugurated as Vice President on April 21, 1789. Washington, arriving later, was inaugurated on April 30, 1789. He was reelected in 1792, and served out the first two presidential terms, but since the first was less than four years long (April 30, 1789–March 4, 1793), he doesn't belong on the list.

George W. Bush was elected in 2000, and then reelected in 2004. If he serves out the remainder of his term, until January 20, 2009, he will be added to this list.

82

The Five Presidents Who Served the Shortest Terms

1. WILLIAM HENRY HARRISON served as President for a scant 31 days. He was inaugurated on a very rainy March 4, 1841, during which he spoke (without a hat or coat) outdoors for almost two hours. He developed pneumonia, and died on April 4, 1841, too soon for his wife to even get to Washington to live in the White House as First Lady.

2. JAMES ABRAM GARFIELD served only 199 days. He took office on March 4, 1881. On July 2, 1881, he was waiting for a train when Charles Guiteau shot him in the back. He didn't die immediately, and for a time seemed to improve, but then died on September 19, 1881.

3. ZACHARY TAYLOR served one year, 127 days. He survived several wars—including the War of 1812, the Black Hawk War, the second Seminole War, and the Mexican-American War of the 1840s—but stomach trouble did him in. He took office on March 4, 1849, and at the very hot July 4, 1850, celebrations, ate cold meat with ice water and milk, which led to a bout of gastroenteritis which in turn brought on the coronary thrombosis that killed him on July 9, 1850.

4. WARREN GAMALIEL HARDING's term lasted two years, 151 days. He took office on March 4, 1921, but was suffering a serious decline in popularity by the middle of 1923, so he went on a grand tour of the western United States in late June. He suffered an attack of food poisoning on July 27, and then died suddenly of cerebral thrombosis on August 2, 1923.

5. GERALD RUDOLPH FORD served two years, 164 days. He is the only President on this list who didn't die in office. He took office on August 9, 1974, following Richard Nixon's resignation, and served out his term. Some say his defeat in the election of 1976 was sealed by his pardon of Nixon, others that there was no way any Republican could have won that election following Nixon's Watergate scandal. At any rate, he left office on January 20, 1977, as Jimmy Carter was inaugurated, and then lived nearly 30 years in retirement.

83

Presidents Who Shared Birthdays/ Death Days with Vice Presidents

FIVE DAYS SAW THE BIRTH OF AT LEAST ONE PRESIDENT AND ONE Vice President, and five different days the death of at least one of each. Truly red letter days include August 27, on which three Vice Presidents (one of whom later became President) were born, and July 4, on which three Presidents and one other Vice President died.

BIRTHDAYS

January 30: President FRANKLIN DELANO ROOSEVELT (1933–45) was born in 1882. Vice President Richard B. "Dick" Cheney (2001–) was born in 1941.

February 6: President RONALD REAGAN (1981–89) was born in 1911. Vice President Aaron Burr (1801–05) was born in 1756.

March 18: President GROVER CLEVELAND (1885–89, 1893–97) was born in 1837. Vice President John C. Calhoun (1825–33) was born in 1782.

August 27: President (and Vice President) LYNDON BAINES JOHNSON (1963–69) was born in 1908. Vice President Hannibal Hamlin (1861–65) was born in 1809. And Vice President Charles G. Dawes (1925–29) was born in 1865.

November 24: President ZACHARY TAYLOR (1849–50) was born in 1784. Vice President Alben W. Barkley (1949–53) was born in 1877.

DEATH DAYS

June 1: President JAMES BUCHANAN (1857–61) died in 1868. Vice President Thomas R. Marshall (1913–21) died in 1925.

July 4: Presidents (and Vice Presidents) JOHN ADAMS (1797–1801) and THOMAS JEFFERSON (1801–09) both died in 1826. President JAMES MONROE (1817–25) died in 1831. Vice President Hannibal Hamlin (1861–65) died in 1891.

September 14: President WILLIAM McKINLEY (1897–1901) died in 1901. Vice President Aaron Burr (1801–05) died in 1836.

November 18: President (and Vice President) CHESTER ALAN ARTHUR (1881–85) died in 1886. Vice President Henry A. Wallace (1941–45) died in 1965.

November 22: President JOHN FITZGERALD KENNEDY (1961–63) died in 1963. Vice President Henry Wilson (1873–75) died in 1875. Both these men died in office.

December 26: President (and Vice President) HARRY TRUMAN died in 1972. President (and Vice President) GERALD FORD died in 2006.

84

Presidents Who Had More Than One Vice President

ALTHOUGH WE ELECT THEM AS A TEAM, THERE IS NO REQUIRE-ment for a President to have only one Vice President. Some Vice Presidents have died in office, others have left for other jobs, and still others have been dropped from the team by their Presidents. For various reasons, the following nine Presidents had more than one Vice President:

1. THOMAS JEFFERSON (1801–09). His first Vice President, Aaron Burr, almost became President in his own right. Jefferson and Burr each received 73 electoral votes (before the adoption of the 12th Amendment, which provided for the joint election of the President and the Vice President). The House of Representatives chose Jefferson for President and Burr for Vice President. Their disagreement, and Burr's refusal to cede the election to Jefferson, caused a rift between them that only widened during their term.

Burr was replaced on the ticket in 1804 with George Clinton, who served two terms as Vice President.

2. JAMES MADISON (1809–17). His first Vice President was George Clinton, who had first been elected to that office under Jefferson. Clinton had designs on the presidential nomination in 1808, but lost it to Madison, and was reelected Vice President. He died in office on April 20, 1812, aged 72.

For Madison's reelection in 1812, Elbridge Gerry was chosen to run for Vice President, in part because he had no designs on the presidency, and Madison's Republican Party was already planning to run James Monroe for President in 1816. Madison and Gerry were elected, but Gerry died in office on November 23, 1814, aged 70.

3. ANDREW JACKSON (1829–37). His first Vice President was John C. Calhoun, who was JOHN QUINCY ADAMS's Vice President from 1825 to 1829. Calhoun and Jackson disagreed on several issues, and Calhoun became the first Vice President to resign, on December 28, 1832, in order to take the Senate seat he'd just been elected to, representing South Carolina.

Jackson had already chosen Martin Van Buren to be his running mate in the election of 1832, and even considered resigning so Van Buren could assume the presidency without an election. Van Buren talked him out of resignation, but was elected to succeed him in 1836.

4. ABRAHAM LINCOLN (1861–65). His first Vice President was Hannibal Hamlin, from Maine. Hamlin was a staunch abolitionist, and they were elected in 1860. In 1864, at the age of 55, Hamlin enlisted as a private in the Maine Coast Guard, and served two months as a cook.

Lincoln dropped Hamlin from the ticket in 1864, in favor of War Democrat Andrew Johnson, who remained loyal to the

Union even though his home state of Tennessee had seceded. Lincoln won reelection with Johnson on the ticket, and then Johnson succeeded to the presidency when Lincoln was assassinated in April 1865.

5. ULYSSES S. GRANT (1869–77). His first Vice President, Schuyler Colfax, was accused of taking a bribe, as were many other congressmen who bought below-market value stock in Crédit Mobilier, which built the Union Pacific Railroad. Colfax was never formally charged, but the accusations damaged his reputation, and Grant dropped him from the ticket in 1872.

Grant replaced him with Henry Wilson for the election, and won reelection with him. Wilson suffered two strokes while serving as Vice President, and died in office on November 22, 1875, aged 63.

6. GROVER CLEVELAND (1885–89, 1893–97). Cleveland's first running mate, Thomas A. Hendricks, had previously run for Vice President in 1876, but lost. In 1880 and 1884 he tried to win the Democratic nomination for President, but settled for the vice presidential spot with Cleveland. Hendricks died of a stroke at the age of 66, on November 25, 1885, having served less than nine months as Vice President.

Cleveland's second running mate and Vice President was Adlai Ewing Stevenson (whose grandson would twice run for the presidency against DWIGHT EISENHOWER, in 1952 and 1956). Stevenson had been Cleveland's assistant postmaster general in his first term. He was also William Jennings Bryan's running mate in 1900, but lost that election.

7. WILLIAM McKINLEY (1897–1901). His first Vice President, Garret A. Hobart, was from New Jersey, and his presence on the ticket may have been part of the reason New Jersey, for the first

time since 1872, voted Republican. Hobart died in office on November 21, 1899, at the age of 55.

For McKinley's reelection, New York's Boss Thomas Platt promoted Theodore Roosevelt as Vice President, in order to remove him from the governorship of New York. Roosevelt wasn't interested in leaving, but was eventually convinced (in large part due to Senator Henry Cabot Lodge's influence), and was elected. McKinley was shot on September 6, 1901, and died on September 13. On September 14, Roosevelt was inaugurated as the youngest man ever to be President.

8. FRANKLIN DELANO ROOSEVELT (1933–45). The only President to serve more than two terms, he was also the only one to have more than two Vice Presidents. His first Vice President, John Nance Garner, was the longest-lived Vice President (he died two weeks before his 99th birthday, in 1967). Garner served for Roosevelt's first two terms, but then broke with him over Roosevelt's plan to pack the Supreme Court, and over his decision to run for a third term. Garner challenged him for the nomination in 1940 and lost.

Henry Agard Wallace was Roosevelt's Secretary of Agriculture before being chosen to run for Vice President in 1940. Wallace's views on postwar international cooperation and foreign aid drew criticism from party leaders, and they persuaded Roosevelt to drop him from the ticket in 1944. Roosevelt appointed Wallace Secretary of Commerce after his term as Vice President, but President Truman fired him. Wallace ran for President in 1948 and got 2.4 percent of the votes cast. His father, Henry C. Wallace, had been Secretary of Agriculture under Presidents Harding and Coolidge.

Roosevelt's third running mate was Harry S Truman, who served only briefly as Vice President. He succeeded to the presidency upon Roosevelt's death on April 12, 1945.

9. RICHARD M. NIXON (1969–74). His first Vice President, Spiro T. Agnew, was the second Vice President to resign. He and Nixon were elected in 1968 and again in 1972, but in August 1973, federal prosecutors announced that Agnew was the target of an investigation involving kickbacks when he was governor of Maryland. Later, they expanded the investigation to include taking bribes as Vice President. Agnew made a deal with the prosecutors in which he would resign and plead no contest to one charge of income tax evasion, which he did. He resigned on October 10, 1973.

Gerald R. Ford was the first Vice President to be appointed to the office, under the provisions of the 25th Amendment. Ford was House Minority Leader at the time Nixon chose him for the job. He was confirmed by the Senate by a vote of 92–3, and by the House, 387–35. He took the oath of office on December 6, 1973. On August 9, 1974, Nixon became the first President to resign, and Ford succeeded him as President.

85

Presidents Who Had No Vice President

Vice Presidents Who Became President

BEFORE THE ADOPTION OF THE 25TH AMENDMENT IN 1967, THERE was no Constitutional provision for filling a vacancy in the vice presidency. As a result, every Vice President who succeeded to the presidency upon the death of his President served without a Vice President for the remainder of that term. There were four: 1. JOHN TYLER (April 4, 1841–March 4, 1845). Having served only

31 days as Vice President when President WILLIAM HENRY HAR-RISON became the first to die in office, he served three years and eleven months without a Vice President.

2. MILLARD FILLMORE (July 10, 1850–March 4, 1853). President ZACHARY TAYLOR died on July 9, 1850, and the next day, Fillmore took the oath of office, leaving the vice presidency vacant until President FRANKLIN PIERCE and Vice President William R. King took office on March 4, 1853.

3. ANDREW JOHNSON (April 15, 1865–March 4, 1869). Johnson served as Vice President slightly longer than John Tyler. President ABRAHAM LINCOLN was assassinated on April 15, 1865, 42 days after he started his second term, which was Johnson's first as Vice President. Johnson had no Vice President for his entire term.

4. CHESTER ALAN ARTHUR (September 20, 1881–March 4, 1885). President James A. Garfield was shot in July 1881, but hung on until September 19. Following his death, Arthur moved up to the presidency on September 20, 1881, leaving the vice presidency vacant until 1885.

Vice Presidents Who Became President and Later Had VPs Elected with Them

In addition to the Presidents who never had a Vice President, the following had no Vice President when they succeeded to the office, but were later elected to their own terms, at which time they had Vice Presidents elected with them.

1. THEODORE ROOSEVELT (September 14, 1901–March 4, 1905). Roosevelt was the youngest man ever to become President when he took the oath of office on September 14, 1901, following President WILLIAM McKINLEY's death from a gunshot wound received

a week earlier. Roosevelt served out the remainder of McKinley's term without a Vice President of his own. Then, in 1904, Roosevelt won election to his own term, with Charles W. Fairbanks as his Vice President. Roosevelt was the first Vice President to succeed to the presidency and then be elected to his own term.

2. CALVIN COOLIDGE (August 3, 1923–March 4, 1925). President WARREN G. HARDING died on August 2, 1923, and Coolidge's father, a justice of the peace, swore him into the presidency on August 3. Coolidge had no Vice President for the remainder of Harding's term, but was elected to his own term in 1924 with Charles G. Dawes as his Vice President.

3. HARRY S TRUMAN (April 12, 1945–January 20, 1949). Truman was President FRANKLIN DELANO ROOSEVELT's third Vice President, and the one who served the shortest term. Roosevelt died April 12, 1945, and Truman succeeded him less than three months after taking office as Vice President. He finished Roosevelt's fourth term without a Vice President, then was elected on his own in 1948, with Alben W. Barkley as his Vice President.

4. LYNDON BAINES JOHNSON (November 22, 1963–January 20, 1965). President JOHN FITZGERALD KENNEDY was assassinated on November 22, 1963, and Johnson became the first President sworn in by a woman—U.S. District Court Judge Sarah T. Hughes, aboard Air Force One—an hour later in Dallas, Texas. He had no Vice President during the remainder of Kennedy's term, but was elected to his own term with Hubert H. Humphrey as his Vice President.

Presidents Whose Vice Presidents Died

Several Presidents came to office with a Vice President, but were then deprived of his services by death.

1. JAMES MADISON (April 20, 1812–March 4, 1813; November 23, 1814–March 4, 1817). Madison was twice unlucky with Vice Presidents. His first, George Clinton (who had also served as Vice President during President THOMAS JEFFERSON's second term), died in office on April 20, 1812. Madison's second, Elbridge Gerry, also died in office, on November 23, 1814.

2. FRANKLIN PIERCE (April 18, 1853–March 4, 1857). Vice President William Rufus DeVane King was terminally ill with tuberculosis when he was chosen as Pierce's running mate. After the election, he went to Cuba seeking relief. And because he was too ill to return to Washington for the inaugural ceremonies, he became the only nationally elected public official to be sworn in on foreign soil. He improved a little, and returned home to Alabama, but was unable to get to Washington to assume his duties as Vice President. He was Vice President for 45 days.

3. GROVER CLEVELAND (November 25, 1885–March 4, 1889). Vice President Thomas A. Hendricks had run unsuccessfully for Vice President in 1876, and tried but failed to get the presidential nomination in 1880 and 1884. He ran as Cleveland's vice presidential running mate in 1884, then died of a stroke on November 25, 1885.

4. WILLIAM McKINLEY (November 21, 1899–March 4, 1901). Vice President Garret Augustus Hobart was only 55 when he died in office, leaving McKinley without a Vice President for the remainder of his first term. McKinley was assassinated in his second term, leaving his second Vice President, Theodore Roosevelt, to succeed him, and he had no Vice President for three and a half more years.

5. WILLIAM HOWARD TAFT (October 30, 1912–March 4, 1913). Vice President James Schoolcraft Sherman was elected with Taft

in 1908, and renominated with Taft in 1912. Sherman died of Bright's disease days before the election, although Taft's loss was virtually assured when his predecessor, Theodore Roosevelt, announced he was running against Taft for another term. Woodrow Wilson won easily over a divided Republican party.

Vice Presidential Gaps

Finally, three Presidents had a vice presidential gap due to resignation; two due to the Vice President resigning, one because the President resigned.

1. ANDREW JACKSON (December 28, 1832–March 4, 1833). Vice President John C. Calhoun had been John Quincy Adams's Vice President, and then was elected to serve with Jackson. However, Jackson and Calhoun had a falling-out, and Calhoun was dropped from the ticket for Jackson's reelection. He resigned on December 28, 1832, two months before his second term was scheduled to end, to take the seat in the Senate to which he'd just been elected.

2. RICHARD NIXON (October 10–December 6, 1973). After twice being elected with Nixon, Vice President Spiro T. Agnew, in a deal with federal prosecutors, pleaded guilty to one charge of income tax evasion and resigned on October 10, 1973. The plea and resignation kept him from facing prosecution for taking bribes as Vice President and a kickback scheme when he was governor of Maryland. Soon thereafter, Nixon chose House Minority Leader Gerald R. Ford as his new Vice President, under the terms of the 25th Amendment. He was confirmed by the Senate (92–3) and the House (387–35), and took the oath of office on December 6, 1973.

3. GERALD FORD (August 9–December 19, 1974). Following President RICHARD NIXON's resignation, Ford assumed the presidency, and again, there was a vacancy in the vice presidency. In line with the 25th Amendment, Ford nominated New York Governor Nelson A. Rockefeller to fill the post, and he was duly confirmed by Congress, and took the oath of office on December 19, 1974.

86

Presidents Defeated in Their Bids for Reelection

OF THE 42 MEN TO BE PRESIDENT, 12 WERE DEFEATED IN THEIR bids for reelection. Only two of these 12 (Fillmore and Ford) were never elected President. Fillmore succeeded upon Taylor's death, Ford upon Nixon's resignation. The other Vice Presidents who succeeded either weren't nominated for their own terms or were subsequently elected.

1. JOHN ADAMS in the election of 1800. As with most things concerning Adams, he pales in comparison to Washington, his predecessor. In this case, Federalist Adams had to suffer from a wave of states' rights agitation, including the nullification of the Alien and Sedition Acts. And when New York's legislature went Republican in early 1800, the new legislature chose the electors who chose Jefferson.

2. JOHN QUINCY ADAMS in 1828. In an election that was truly a personality contest (since both candidates basically agreed on the

major issues), war hero Andrew Jackson, who rose from such humble beginnings, soundly defeated the experienced, reserved, upper-crust President.

3. MARTIN VAN BUREN in 1840. Van Buren lost a media-driven election, in large part because of the Panic of 1837 and the accompanying depression. William Henry Harrison (a very well-off man) was portrayed as a poor frontiersman, an image that resonated with voters and defeated Van Buren's New York wealth.

4. MILLARD FILLMORE in 1856. Fillmore was President from Zachary Taylor's death in 1850 until the end of the term, 1853. He wasn't nominated for his own term, and left for a tour of Europe in 1855. While there, he received word that the American Party (also known as the Know-Nothings) had nominated him for President, and he returned for the campaign. He won 21 percent of the vote, but only one state (Maryland), coming in third behind winner Democrat James Buchanan and Republican John C. Frémont.

5. GROVER CLEVELAND in 1888. In a very quiet campaign, Cleveland seemed almost aloof, making only one appearance (when he accepted the nomination for another term). He won the popular vote by 100,000 votes (out of 11 million), but lost the electoral vote when Tammany Hall, the political machine in his home state of New York, worked against him, because he was a reformer. Benjamin Harrison won the electoral vote, 233–168.

6. BENJAMIN HARRISON in 1892. In another rather quiet campaign, Harrison's support of the protectionist McKinley Tariff, which was very unpopular, was the key to the election. Following the sudden death of Mrs. Harrison in October, the candidates ceased campaigning, and former President Grover Cleveland triumphed.

·7 and 8. THEODORE ROOSEVELT and WILLIAM HOWARD TAFT in 1912. Roosevelt served out McKinley's term following his death in 1901, won his own term in 1904, and stepped aside in 1908 for his handpicked successor, William Howard Taft. In 1910 he returned from an African safari displeased with Taft's turn toward conservatism, and in 1912 challenged him for the Republican nomination. Taft won the nomination, so Roosevelt formed the Progressive—or Bull Moose—Party, and ran against Taft and Democrat Woodrow Wilson. Roosevelt's move split the Republican Party, and virtually assured Wilson the election. Wilson won the popular vote 42 to 27 percent, with Taft taking 23 percent and Socialist Eugene V. Debs six percent. In the electoral college, Wilson got 435 votes, Roosevelt 88, and Taft eight.

9. HERBERT HOOVER in 1932. Following the crash of the stock market in late 1929 and the ensuing Great Depression, Hoover's defeat was almost assured. Franklin Delano Roosevelt beat him handily, 57 to 40 percent in the popular vote, and 472 electoral votes to Hoover's 59.

10. GERALD FORD in 1976. Ford succeeded to the presidency upon Richard Nixon's resignation in 1974. Having been appointed Vice President after Spiro Agnew's resignation, Ford was the only President never elected to either office. A month after Nixon's resignation, Ford pardoned him, to save the country from the divisive effects of a protracted trial. Ford started the campaign down 30 points to Jimmy Carter, but managed to close the gap. However, he lost the election, 50 to 48 percent. He won 240 electoral votes to Carter's 297 (Ronald Reagan got one).

11. JIMMY CARTER in 1980. Carter battled inflation and a gasoline shortage, but 52 American hostages taken from the U.S. Embassy in Tehran and held for 444 days was just too much for him to overcome. Ronald Reagan's sunny "everything will be fine" cam-

paign strategy, along with his attacks on Carter's unfulfilled election promises, were enough to give Reagan the election with 51 percent of the popular vote to Carter's 41 percent (third-party candidate John Anderson took 7 percent). In the electoral college, Reagan won 489 votes to Carter's 49.

12. GEORGE H.W. BUSH in 1992. After eight years as Reagan's Vice President, and then four years as his own man, Bush succumbed to a younger, vigorous Bill Clinton, Clinton's massive media support, and independent candidate H. Ross Perot. Some say part of Bush's defeat was founded in bad economic news that was rampant in September and October, and which, two weeks after election day, was found to have started improving four weeks earlier. Nevertheless, Clinton won 43 percent of the popular vote to Bush's 37 percent (Perot took 19 percent). In the electoral college, it was Clinton, 370; Bush, 168.

87

Presidents Who Won Reelection

OF THE 42 MEN TO HOLD THE OFFICE OF PRESIDENT, 16 WERE elected to the post twice. Four more succeeded to the office and then were elected to their own terms, thus being reelected without first being elected (see second list).

1. GEORGE WASHINGTON in 1792. As the first President, of course, he doesn't fit neatly on any list. In this case, he won the vote of every elector in the elections of both 1789 and 1792.

2. THOMAS JEFFERSON in 1804. He was a popular President running against a candidate from the dying Federalist party. It wasn't close, and Jefferson won the electoral vote, 162 to 14.

3. JAMES MADISON in 1812. There was some concern over Madison's handling of the War of 1812. His opponent, DeWitt Clinton (the Federalist-backed Republican) told the hawks that he'd press for a more vigorous prosecution of the war, and the doves that he'd press for peace. In the end, not many of them believed him, and Madison was reelected.

4. JAMES MONROE in 1820. Monroe had such broad support, and the Federalist Party was just about dead (although nothing else had arisen to replace it), that he ran unopposed for reelection. Of the 231 electors, Monroe received 230 votes. The one who did not vote for him was Governor William Plumer of New Hampshire. Legend says he did it to preserve Washington's record as the only unanimously elected President, but a biography of Plumer (written by his son) notes that he didn't like Monroe, and voted for John Quincy Adams in earnest.

5. ANDREW JACKSON in 1832. The Bank of the United States was the key campaign issue in Jackson's reelection. He vetoed its recharter because he thought it unconstitutional. Many people thought it elitist, and Jackson's apparent siding with them carried the tide, and reelection.

6. ABRAHAM LINCOLN in 1864. With the southern states in secession, the Republican Party changed its name to the National Union Party in order to accommodate southern Democrats (such as Vice Presidential candidate Andrew Johnson), and Lincoln was reelected with 55 percent of the popular vote, 212 of the 233 electoral votes cast (22 of the 25 states that voted).

7. ULYSSES GRANT in 1872. President Grant's prestige as a war hero, untainted by the scandals that rocked his administration's

first term, virtually assured his reelection, and he took 56 percent of the popular vote and received 286 electoral votes. His opponent, Horace Greeley, died after the general election, but before the electoral votes were cast, so the 66 votes he would have won were divided amongst four others.

8. GROVER CLEVELAND in 1892. In a quiet campaign, Benjamin Harrison's support of the unpopular protectionist McKinley Tariff was the key to the election. Following the sudden death of Mrs. Harrison in October, the candidates ceased campaigning, and former President Grover Cleveland triumphed, becoming the only man to be defeated in his bid for reelection and then later elected.

9. WILLIAM McKINLEY in 1900. McKinley left most of the campaigning to his new running mate, the young and vigorous Theodore Roosevelt, who toured the country stressing "Four Years More of the Full Dinner Pail." McKinley beat William Jennings Bryan for the second time in a row.

10. WOODROW WILSON in 1916. Following his win in 1912 over the split Republican Party, Wilson ran on the "He Kept Us Out of War" slogan in 1916 (World War I had been raging in Europe since 1914). The election was close, with Republican Charles Evans Hughes enjoying the support of Theodore Roosevelt, the Progressives who came with him, and Catholics protesting Wilson's policy toward Catholic Mexico. Hughes was the leader during the campaign, and expected to win, but late returns from California tipped the scales, and Wilson won 49 percent of the popular vote, and 277 electoral votes to Hughes's 254.

11. FRANKLIN DELANO ROOSEVELT in 1936, 1940, and 1944. A vigorous campaign of public works and public assistance during the Great Depression gave Roosevelt a huge margin of victory in his

first bid for reelection. He won 61 percent of the popular vote, and 523 of the 531 electoral votes.

In 1940, the two major issues were World War II (the United States was not yet involved) and Roosevelt's bid for an unprecedented third term. Roosevelt's opponent, Wendell Wilkie, agreed with most of Roosevelt's domestic policies, and so concentrated on his violation of Washington's two term precedent. Roosevelt still won 55 percent of the popular vote, and 449 of the 531 electoral votes.

In 1944, the country was in the midst of World War II. Republican Thomas E. Dewey refused to attack the administration's foreign policy during wartime, and instead campaigned indirectly against Roosevelt's failing health. It wasn't enough. Roosevelt won 53 percent of the popular vote, and 432 of the electoral votes.

12. DWIGHT EISENHOWER in 1956. Eisenhower was a very popular incumbent, and he'd already beaten his opponent, Adlai Stevenson, in 1952. The 1956 campaign had no major issues, and Eisenhower won by an even bigger margin than in 1952.

13. RICHARD NIXON in 1972. Nixon's opponent, George McGovern, was portrayed in the media as a radical leftist because he called for immediate withdrawal from Vietnam. McGovern also had running-mate troubles, when it was revealed that his first choice, Thomas Eagleton, had undergone electric shock therapy for mental depression. After backing Eagleton, McGovern eventually dumped him for Sargent Shriver, but couldn't get any electoral traction. Nixon won 61 percent of the popular vote and 520 of the 538 electoral votes.

14. RONALD REAGAN in 1984. Reagan was incredibly popular, and his opponent, Walter Mondale, the dour former Vice President, could not make any headway against him. It seemed nothing could stop Reagan's reelection landslide, and he won 59

percent of the popular vote and 525 of the electoral votes (Mondale won only his home state of Minnesota and the District of Columbia).

15. BILL CLINTON in 1996. Republican candidate Bob Dole couldn't appeal to younger voters, and H. Ross Perot's second candidacy helped Clinton's reelection. He took 50 percent of the popular vote, and won the electoral vote 379–159 over Dole.

16. GEORGE W. BUSH in 2004. Bush won the 2000 election in the electoral college, and, some say, in the Supreme Court, although Vice President Al Gore won the popular votes. In 2004, Bush won the popular vote by more than 3 million (out of about 115 million). He won the electoral college, 286–252.

Vice Presidents Who Succeeded to the Presidency and Then Won Their Own Terms

1. THEODORE ROOSEVELT in 1904. Roosevelt and his opponent, Alton B. Parker, agreed on most of the major issues, so the campaign turned into a popularity contest. Roosevelt was much more personable, and since neither candidate campaigned much—Roosevelt stayed in the White House, presumably at work; Parker conducted a passive "front-porch" campaign—Roosevelt won easily.

2. CALVIN COOLIDGE in 1924. Following Warren Harding's death in 1923, Coolidge became President. During his brief term, he was able to restore the public's perception of integrity in the Executive Branch, which, combined with peace and prosperity, was reflected in the campaign slogan "Keep Cool with Coolidge." Coolidge took 54 percent of the popular vote (to Democrat John W. Davis's 29 percent and Progressive Robert M. LaFollette's 17 percent).

3. HARRY TRUMAN in 1948. Truman wasn't expected to win his own term (he wasn't even expected to win the Democratic nomination), and one of the most famous political photographs in history shows Truman holding the *Chicago Tribune* with its DEWEY DEFEATS TRUMAN headline. But some of that expectation was due to the unrefined methods of political polling of the time; among other things, people were telephoned, ignoring the fact that telephones were only standard in the homes of the wealthy. In the end, Truman won 49 percent of the popular vote to Dewey's 45 percent (third-party candidates Strom Thurmond and Henry A. Wallace each took two percent). The electoral vote was 303 for Truman, 189 for Dewey, 39 for Thurmond, and none for Wallace.

4. LYNDON JOHNSON in 1964. Succeeding to office upon the assassination of the popular John Kennedy, Johnson continued most of his policies. The public perception of Barry Goldwater as a radical, out of the popular mainstream, led to a Johnson landslide. He won 61 percent of the popular vote, and 486 of the 538 electoral votes.

88

One-Term Presidents Who Did Not Seek Reelection or Were Denied the Nomination

THE PRESIDENCY MAY BE THE GREATEST JOB IN THE WORLD TO retire from; sometimes it's a puzzle as to why any President would seek reelection. But very few of them take this advice. Of the 42 men to serve as President, only five chose to retire after one term. Two others sought nomination for another term, but were denied by their party.

1. JOHN TYLER (1841–45) succeeded to the presidency—the first Vice President to do so—upon the death of William Henry Harrison. Later that year, he split with his party, the Whigs, over the issue of a national bank. He vetoed two bills to create a third Bank of the United States, which the Whigs favored. In protest, his entire cabinet, except Secretary of State Daniel Webster, resigned in September 1841. Tyler was therefore a President without a party, and denied nomination in his own right in 1844.

Rather than run on a third-party ticket, he supported James Polk, who agreed with him on the annexation of Texas. In April 1844, Tyler had approved a treaty annexing Texas, but the Senate would not ratify it. Following Polk's election on a platform that included the annexation, a joint Congressional resolution was adopted bringing Texas into the Union. Tyler retired from the presidency and returned home to Virginia to start his second family (he married his second wife while serving as President, the first President to get married in office). In February 1861, he was chairman of a convention of 21 states in Washington seeking to stave off the Civil War, but the convention was unsuccessful. Tyler urged Virginia to secede, and served as a member of the Provisional Congress of the Confederacy. In November 1861, he was elected to the Confederate House of Representatives, but died before taking his seat.

2. JAMES POLK (1845–49), during the election of 1844, announced that if elected, he would serve only one term and not seek a second. He was in fact elected, and kept his promise. At age 49, Polk was the youngest President elected to that time. On the day of his retirement (March 4, 1849) he wrote in his diary, "I feel exceed-

ingly relieved that I am now free from all public cares. I am sure I shall be a happier man in my retirement than I have been during the four years I have filled the highest office in the gift of my countrymen." Polk died three months later, on June 15, 1849, having fallen ill on the extensive tour of the southern states he took on his way home from Washington.

3. JAMES BUCHANAN (1857–61) was morally opposed to slavery, but could find no legal opposition to it in the Constitution, and therefore felt forced to support it. His appointment of a southerner as governor of the Kansas Territory only fanned the flames of Bleeding Kansas (the debate over whether the territory would be admitted as a slave or free state). The Panic of 1857 caused a great depression, which Buchanan (following the conventional wisdom) did nothing to alleviate. In the end, he chose not to seek reelection. He led a very private retirement in Pennsylvania, and wrote *Mr. Buchanan's Administration on the Eve of Rebellion*, a self-defense of his actions, which was published in 1866.

4. RUTHERFORD HAYES (1877–81), when accepting the nomination for President in 1876, renounced a second term. He spent the 12 years of his retirement in Ohio, and served as a director of the George Peabody Educational Fund and the John F. Slater Fund, as a trustee of Ohio State University, and as president of the National Prison Association.

5. CHESTER ARTHUR (1881–85). After succeeding to the presidency following James Garfield's death, Arthur changed his views to favor governmental reform. This alienated most of the Republican Party, and denied him the nomination in 1884 for his own term. Arthur spent the two and a half years of his retirement in New York. He served as president of the New York Arcade Railway Company, and resumed practicing law, but his declining health prevented him from doing much.

Two Presidents who sought reelection but were denied their party's nomination:

1. FRANKLIN PIERCE (1853–57). During his term of office, he played a major role in passing the Kansas-Nebraska Act (which repealed the Missouri Compromise). Following its adoption, which allowed settlers in Kansas and Nebraska to determine for themselves whether they would be slave or free states, Pierce was blamed for being unable to maintain order in what became known as Bleeding Kansas. For these actions, he was deemed unelectable by his own Democratic Party, and denied renomination. He spent his 12 years of retirement financially secure, but emotionally strained, in New Hampshire. As the Civil War approached, he spoke out in favor of the South, and later denounced the war policy of President Lincoln. His antiwar sentiments made him very unpopular at home.

2. ANDREW JOHNSON (1865–69). After succeeding to the Presidency following Abraham Lincoln's assassination, Johnson had no party to protect him. A Democrat elected with the Republican Lincoln (on the National Union ticket), following the conclusion of the Civil War, he favored a lenient policy of Reconstruction. The Republican Party had other ideas. In 1867, Johnson vetoed the Tenure of Office Act, which would not allow him to fire Cabinet members without Senate approval. Congress overrode his veto. In February 1868, he fired Secretary of War Edwin Stanton, who as a staunch Republican had been undermining his policies. Johnson was impeached, but acquitted (the vote was 35–19 against, one vote short of the two-thirds required for conviction).

Johnson received a few votes for nomination at the Democratic convention of 1868, but had no real hope of being nominated for his own term, and retired in 1869. During the six years of his retirement in Tennessee, he remained active in the Democratic Party. He ran unsuccessfully for the Senate in 1871 and the House in 1872. In 1875, the Tennessee legislature elected him to the U.S. Senate, and he became the only former President to serve in the Senate. He made only one floor speech, in March 1875, denouncing the Grant administration's Reconstruction policy. He died July 31, 1875.

89

Presidents Inaugurated Outside Washington, D.C.

TWO PRESIDENTS (GEORGE WASHINGTON AND JOHN ADAMS) WERE inaugurated before Washington, D.C., became the seat of government. They were the only Presidents inaugurated in the capital, but not in Washington. Since the national capital moved to Washington, D.C., in 1800, the only Presidents inaugurated anywhere else were Vice Presidents who succeeded to the presidency upon the sudden death of the President.

1. GEORGE WASHINGTON. When the Constitution was adopted and the new federal government was organized, the nation's capital was New York City. Following Washington's election on February 4, 1789, he took some time getting to the capital, and was inaugurated there on April 30, 1789, on the balcony of Federal Hall. At the end of 1790, the seat of government moved to Philadelphia, and following Washington's reelection, he was inaugurated again in the Senate Chamber of the new Federal Hall, in Philadelphia, on March 4, 1793.

2. JOHN ADAMS. Following his election as the second President, he was inaugurated in the House of Representatives Chamber of Federal Hall in Philadelphia, which was still the national capital.

3. CHESTER ARTHUR. Arthur learned of the death of James Garfield about 11:30 P.M. on September 19, 1881 (about an hour after he died). Arthur was sworn in to the presidency in his own house, 123 Lexington Avenue, New York City, at 2:15 A.M. on September 20, 1881 (New York Supreme Court Justice John R. Brady administered the oath). Two days later, after returning to Washington, he again took the oath of office in a private ceremony in the Vice President's room in the Capitol, this time administered by Chief Justice Morrison R. Waite.

4. THEODORE ROOSEVELT. Upon the death of William McKinley on September 14, 1901, Roosevelt was inaugurated by Judge John R. Hazel of the U.S. District Court in Buffalo, New York. He then won the election of 1904 and was inaugurated again on the Constitutionally mandated date, March 4, 1905, in Washington, D.C., by Chief Justice Melville W. Fuller.

5. CALVIN COOLIDGE. Visiting his father in Vermont when Warren Harding died suddenly on August 2, 1923, he was inaugurated by his father, a justice of the peace, in the early hours of August 3. He again took the oath of office on August 21, 1923, in his hotel suite in Washington, when it was administered by Justice Adolph August Hoehling of the District of Columbia Supreme Court. Coolidge then won the election of 1924 and was inaugurated again on March 4, 1925, by Chief Justice (and former President) William Howard Taft in the capital.

6. LYNDON BAINES JOHNSON. Upon the death of John F. Kennedy on November 22, 1963, Johnson was inaugurated by Judge Sarah T. Hughes aboard Air Force One on the ground at Love Field in Dallas. Hughes, a judge of the U.S. District Court for the North-

ern District of Texas, was the first woman to administer the oath of office to a President. Johnson won the election of 1964 and was again inaugurated on January 20, 1965, with Chief Justice Earl Warren administering the oath at the Capitol.

90

The Five Presidents Who Issued the Most Vetoes

THE PRESIDENTIAL VETO IS ONE OF THE CHECKS AND BALANCES that makes the three-part U.S. government such a steady institution. Congress (the Legislative branch) adopts bills, but the President must sign them for them to become laws. Alternately, the President can veto bills, checking the Congress's power to make laws.

The presidential veto was very rarely used in the early years of the Republic: Only ten were issued in the first 50 years. Ulysses Grant issued the 100th veto more than 80 years after George Washington took office, Woodrow Wilson issued the 1000th about 50 years later, and Harry Truman issued the 2000th about 45 years after that. Bill Clinton's last veto was the 2,551st.

1. FRANKLIN ROOSEVELT (1933–45) vetoed 635 bills during his 12 years in office (372 signed vetoes, and 263 pocket vetoes). That was an average of 53 vetoes per year, or 4.4 per month. And yet his political party, the Democrats, were in control of Congress for his entire term of office.

2. GROVER CLEVELAND vetoed 414 bills during his first term of office (1885–89), of which 304 were signed and 110 were pocket. During his second term (1893–97), he vetoed another 170 bills (42 signed, 128 pocket), for a total of 584 vetoes during eight years (73 per year, or 6.1 per month). If each term is counted separately, his first term would still be second on this list, and his second term would be fifth.

3. HARRY TRUMAN (1945–53) vetoed 250 bills in less than eight years (180 signed and 70 pocket). He averaged 31.25 vetoes per year, or 2.7 per month. And the 20-year period of Roosevelt and Truman's administrations saw 885 vetoes, more than one-third of all the vetoes issued between 1789 and 2000.

4. DWIGHT EISENHOWER (1953–61) vetoed 181 bills in his eight years in office—73 signed and 108 pocket—giving him an average of 22.63 vetoes per year, or 1.9 per month.

5. ULYSSES S. GRANT (1869–77) vetoed more bills in his eight years in office than had been vetoed by all the previous Presidents combined. He vetoed 93 bills (45 signed, 48 pocket), compared to his predecessors' 87 (57 signed, 30 pocket). That worked out to 11.63 per year, or 0.97 per month.

Obviously, one of the determinants in number of vetoes is time in office, but if we were looking at average vetoes per year, we'd have to jump Gerald Ford (1974–77) onto the list. Though he only served two years and five months, he vetoed 66 bills (48 signed, 18 pocket), for an average of 26.4 per year, or 2.3 per month.

The Presidents Who Issued the Fewest Vetoes

WHILE THE PRESIDENT HAS THE ABILITY TO VETO BILLS FROM Congress, there is no requirement that he use this power, and several Presidents have not felt the need.

The veto was very rarely used in the early days of the Republic. In the 40 years after Washington was inaugurated, only ten bills were vetoed.

There were seven Presidents who chose not to veto any bills (though admittedly, several of them didn't have the time). They were: John Adams (1797–1801), Thomas Jefferson (1801–09), John Quincy Adams (1825–29), William Henry Harrison (March–April 1841), Zachary Taylor (1849–50), Millard Fillmore (1850–53), and James Garfield (March–September 1881).

Two Presidents who each vetoed one bill: James Monroe (1817–25) and Martin Van Buren (1837–41).

George Washington (1789–97) vetoed two bills, and James Polk (1845–49) vetoed three.

The Five Presidents Who Had the Most Vetoes Overridden

WHILE THE SYSTEM OF CHECKS AND BALANCES GIVES THE PRESI-
dent power over Congress in the form of either signing or veto-
ing legislation, it also gives Congress the power to override a
presidential veto by a two-thirds vote. This rarely happens, as
many Presidents are savvy enough to realize when a measure is
so popular that Congress will be able to override a veto.

Of the 2,551 vetoes issued through the end of Bill Clinton's
term, only 106 have subsequently been overridden by Congress
(less than 4.2 percent). The three most overridden Presidents all
succeeded to the office, rather than being elected (although one
of them was later elected to his own term). The five are:

1. ANDREW JOHNSON (1865–69), 15 overrides. Johnson succeeded
following Abraham Lincoln's assassination, and served nearly all
of Lincoln's second term. In nearly four years, he vetoed 29 bills,
half as many as all of his predecessors combined—Johnson was
constantly at odds with Congress. Fifteen of his vetoes (51.7 percent) were overridden.

2 (tie). GERALD FORD (1974–77), 12 overrides. Ford succeeded to the presidency following Richard Nixon's resignation, and had to contend with a hostile Congress, even as he tried to heal the wounds caused by Nixon's actions. He vetoed 66 bills in his two and a half years in office (which puts him close to the top of the list of most bills vetoed). Congress responded by overriding 12 of his vetoes (18.2 percent, or nearly five per year).

2 (tie). HARRY TRUMAN (1945–53), 12 overrides. Truman succeeded following Franklin Roosevelt's death, and then was elected to his own term. In nearly eight years in office, his vetoes were overridden 12 times . . . but he vetoed 250 bills, giving him a 95.2 percent success rate.

4 (tie). RONALD REAGAN (1981–89), nine overrides. Reagan's party, the Republicans, controlled the Senate until 1987, but the Democrats had control of the House his entire term of office. Reagan's popularity, however, gave him some control over legislation, and he only vetoed 78 bills during his eight years in office. The nine overridden by Congress amounts to 11.5 percent.

4 (tie). FRANKLIN DELANO ROOSEVELT (1933–45), nine overrides. The number, over a span of 12 years in office, seems remarkably smaller when compared to his total number of vetoes: 635. That means only 1.4 percent of his vetoes were overridden.

In terms of percentage, Franklin Pierce (1853–57) leads the list, with 55.6 percent of his vetoes overridden. Although in absolute numbers, that translates into five overrides of nine vetoes.

Twelve of the Presidents who vetoed bills (and have completed their terms at this writing) had none of their vetoes overridden. The most successful of these was William McKinley, who vetoed 42 bills.

93

The Six Presidents Inaugurated
on Two Different Days

1. GEORGE WASHINGTON. Following the signing of the Constitution (on September 17, 1787), and its ratification by nine states
(New Hampshire was the ninth state to ratify, on June 21, 1788,
bringing it into effect), the election of the first President under
the Constitution began. The balloting took place on February 4,
1789, and Washington received all 69 electoral votes (from the
ten states voting). After being notified of his election, he did not
hurry to New York City, the national capital. He was sworn in at
Federal Hall on April 30, 1789, by Robert R. Livingston, chancellor of the state of New York, nine days after Vice President
John Adams. Following Washington's reelection, he was inaugurated in the new capital, Philadelphia, by Associate Justice
William Cushing. This inauguration took place on March 4,
1793.

2. THEODORE ROOSEVELT. Upon the death of William McKinley
on September 14, 1901, Roosevelt was inaugurated by Judge
John R. Hazel of the U.S. District Court in Buffalo, New York.
He then won the election of 1904 and was inaugurated again on
the Constitutionally mandated date, March 4, 1905, by Chief
Justice Melville W. Fuller.

3. CALVIN COOLIDGE. Visiting his father in Vermont when Warren Harding died suddenly on August 2, 1923, Coolidge was inaugurated by his father, a justice of the peace, in the early hours of August 3. He again took the oath of office on August 21 in his hotel suite in Washington, when it was administered by Justice Adolph August Hoehling of the District of Columbia Supreme Court. Coolidge then won the election of 1924 and was inaugurated again on March 4, 1925, by Chief Justice (and former President) William Howard Taft.

4. FRANKLIN DELANO ROOSEVELT. Upon winning the election of 1932, he was inaugurated on March 4, 1933, by Chief Justice Charles Evans Hughes. The 20th Amendment to the Constitution (ratified in 1933) changed inauguration day to January 20, so after Roosevelt's reelection in 1936, he was inaugurated on that date. Hughes again administered the oath, as he did on January 20, 1940. For Roosevelt's fourth and final inaugural, on January 20, 1944, newly appointed Chief Justice Harlan Fiske Stone administered the oath of office.

5. HARRY S TRUMAN. Upon Roosevelt's death three months after his fourth inauguration, Truman was inaugurated on April 12, 1945, in the Cabinet Room of the White House by Chief Justice Harlan Fiske Stone. He later won the election of 1948, and was again inaugurated on January 20, 1949, at the Capitol by Chief Justice Frederick Moore Vinson.

6. LYNDON BAINES JOHNSON. Upon the death of John F. Kennedy on November 22, 1963, Johnson was inaugurated by Judge Sarah T. Hughes aboard Air Force One on the ground at Love Field in Dallas. Hughes, a judge of the U.S. District Court for the Northern District of Texas, was the first woman to administer the oath of office to a President. Johnson won the election of 1964 and was again inaugurated on January 20, 1965,

with Chief Justice Earl Warren administering the oath at the Capitol.

94

Gaps When There Was No President

CONSTITUTIONALLY, THE PRESIDENT'S TERM OF OFFICE ENDS AT noon on January 20 in the year after an election year (this date was changed from March 4 during Franklin Roosevelt's term of office). The inauguration of the new President is timed to maintain the office. And since the advent of near-instantaneous communication (and even before), finding the Vice President in cases where the President has died in office have occasioned very little delay. The largest gaps when there was no President occurred before George Washington was sworn in as the first, and following the first presidential death in office, William Henry Harrison, when word had to be carried to the Vice President on horseback.

1. Until April 30, 1789. The Constitution was signed on September 17, 1787, and came into effect following ratification by New Hampshire (the ninth state to ratify) on June 21, 1788. Under this new system of government, there was much to do, including choosing the first President. The balloting took place on February 4, 1789, at which time, GEORGE WASHINGTON received all 69 electoral votes from the ten states voting (New York was unable to decide which electors to send, and neither North Carolina nor

Rhode Island had yet ratified the Constitution). Washington was notified of his election, but took some time getting to New York City, which was the national capital. Vice President–elect John Adams arrived on April 21, 1789, and was duly sworn in. Washington arrived on April 30, at which time Chancellor Robert R. Livingston of the state of New York administered the oath. So there was no President until April 30, 1789 (excepting those who were President under the Articles of Confederation, see "About Washington's Predecessors").

2. April 4, 1841 (12:30 A.M.)–April 6, 1841. WILLIAM HENRY HARRISON caught pneumonia while giving a long inaugural speech in bad weather on March 4, 1841. He died just after midnight on April 4, 1841, having served one month. Vice President John Tyler had not been kept informed of Harrison's worsening condition, so he was surprised when the chief clerk of the State Department, Fletcher Webster, woke him early on April 5 at his home in Williamsburg, Virginia, with the news of Harrison's death. Tyler left for Washington, arriving the next day, where Chief Justice William Cranch of the U.S. Circuit Court of the District of Columbia, swore him in.

3. July 9, 1850 (12:35 P.M.)–July 10, 1850 (12:00 P.M.). Vice President Millard Fillmore visited President ZACHARY TAYLOR early on July 9, and realized he was dying, so he wasn't surprised when a White House messenger visited his room at the Willard Hotel in Washington later that day to tell him that Taylor had died. At noon the next day, William Cranch, who had sworn in President Tyler nine years earlier, administered the oath to Fillmore in front of a joint session of Congress.

4. April 15, 1865. Just a few hours elapsed between President ABRAHAM LINCOLN's death at 7:22 A.M. and Chief Justice Salmon P. Chase swearing in Vice President Andrew Johnson to succeed him.

5. September 19, 1881 (10:35 P.M.)–September 20, 1881 (2:15 A.M.). Less than four hours elapsed between President JAMES GARFIELD's death from the gunshot wounds he'd received two months earlier and Vice President Chester Arthur's taking the oath of office administered by New York Supreme Court Justice John R. Brady. A messenger arrived at Arthur's home about 11:30 with the news. This was only a brief gap, but at the time he was sworn in, there was no Vice President, and also no President pro tempore of the Senate nor Speaker of the House (Congress was not in session, and had not selected either officer yet), so there was no Constitutional line of succession should something happen to Arthur. Mindful of the danger this posed, President Arthur drafted a proclamation calling the Senate into special session, and mailed it to the White House. Once he safely arrived in Washington, he destroyed the letter and called the Senate into session. On September 22, he took the oath of office again, this time administered by Chief Justice Morrison R. Waite.

6. September 14, 1901. On September 13, a week after President WILLIAM MCKINLEY had been shot in Buffalo, New York, Vice President Theodore Roosevelt was informed that the President was dying. (He had visited earlier in the week, when McKinley seemed to be improving, and then returned to his family vacation in the Adirondacks.) Roosevelt rushed back to Buffalo, but arrived after McKinley's death at 2:15 A.M. U.S. District Court Judge John R. Hazel swore Roosevelt into office later that day.

7. August 2, 1923 (10:30 P.M. Eastern Time)–August 3, 1923 (2:47 A.M.). President WARREN HARDING died of what was assumed to be a stroke about 7:30 P.M. in his hotel room in San Francisco, California, at the end of a long, sometimes strenuous tour of the western states. Vice President Calvin Coolidge, visiting his father in Plymouth Notch, Vermont, was informed of Harding's death by his stenographer, Erwin C. Geisser; his

chauffeur, Joseph N. McInerney; and reporter William H. Crawford. Coolidge's father, a justice of the peace and notary public, administered the oath of office to his son at 2:47 A.M. in his sitting room, after which now–President Coolidge went back to sleep. After returning to Washington, Justice Adolph August Hoehling of the D.C. Supreme Court again administered the oath of office on August 21.

8. April 12, 1945. President FRANKLIN ROOSEVELT died of a cerebral hemorrhage in Warm Springs, Georgia, at 3:35 P.M. Vice President Harry Truman was visiting with Speaker of the House Sam Rayburn when he was summoned to the White House, where Eleanor Roosevelt told him the President was dead. At 7:09 P.M., Chief Justice Harlan Fiske Stone swore Truman in as President in the White House Cabinet Room.

9. November 22, 1963. President JOHN KENNEDY was shot while traveling in a motorcade in Dallas, Texas, about 12:30 P.M., and was pronounced dead half an hour later. Vice President Lyndon Johnson, who had been two cars behind Kennedy in the motorcade, was sworn in at 2:39 P.M. aboard Air Force One, which was sitting on the ground at Love Field in Dallas. U.S. District Court Judge Sarah T. Hughes administered the oath, becoming the first woman to swear in a President of the United States.

95

The Presidents Who Saw the Most States Join the Union

THE CONSTITUTION WAS SIGNED IN 1787, AND CAME INTO EFFECT on June 21, 1788, when New Hampshire became the ninth state to ratify it. The electors of the several states met to choose the first President on February 4, 1789, by which time Virginia and New York had also ratified the Constitution (although New York didn't choose electors to vote for President). Following George Washington's inauguration, North Carolina and Rhode Island became the last of the original 13 colonies to ratify the Constitution. Following those 13, another 37 states joined the Union.

1. BENJAMIN HARRISON (1889–93). Six states joined the Union during his four-year term: North Dakota and South Dakota (on November 2, 1889), Montana (November 8, 1889), Washington (November 11, 1889), Idaho (July 3, 1890), and Wyoming (July 10, 1890).

2 (tie). GEORGE WASHINGTON (1789–97). Following the original 13, five more states joined the Union during Washington's eight years as President: North Carolina (November 21, 1789), Rhode Island (May 29, 1790), Vermont (March 4, 1791), Kentucky (June 1, 1792), and Tennessee (June 1, 1796).

218 THE PRESIDENTIAL BOOK OF LISTS

2 (tie). JAMES MONROE (1817–25). Only three new states joined the Union between Washington's term and Monroe's (between 1797 and 1817), then five joined during Monroe's eight-year term: Mississippi (December 10, 1817), Illinois (December 3, 1818), Alabama (December 14, 1819), Maine (March 15, 1820), and Missouri (August 10, 1821).

4 (tie). JAMES POLK (1845–49). Three states joined the Union during James Polk's four-year term, the 28th, 29th, and 30th states: Texas (December 29, 1845), Iowa (December 28, 1846), and Wisconsin (May 29, 1848).

4 (tie). JAMES BUCHANAN (1857–61). The last three states to join the Union before the start of the Civil War were during Buchanan's administration: Minnesota (May 11, 1858), Oregon (February 14, 1859), and Kansas (January 29, 1861). In between Oregon and Kansas, however, six southern states (South Carolina, Mississippi, Florida, Alabama, Georgia, and Louisiana) seceded from the Union, rejoining after the end of the war.

96

The Presidents Involved in Wars During Their Terms

THE UNITED STATES HAS BEEN ENGAGED IN MANY WARS, MOST OF them successfully. Indeed, almost half of the Presidents have served during wartime. Some wars were larger or more consuming than others, but all were wars, resulting in loss of life and property (except for Van Buren's Aroostook War, which was bloodless).

1. GEORGE WASHINGTON: During the first presidential administration, and continuing into the 1840s, the United States fought skirmishes, battles, and wars with the native Indians.

2. THOMAS JEFFERSON: Tripolitan War (1801–05), against the pirates of Morocco, Algiers, Tripoli, and Tunis (also known as the Barbary States). The United States won a qualified victory.

3. JAMES MADISON: War of 1812 (1812–14), against Great Britain. The war ended in pretty much a stalemate, although it did mark the emergence of the United States as a truly independent nation, ending its economic dependence on Britain. It brought General Andrew Jackson to prominence, when he led a decisive victory over the British at New Orleans in January 1815 (which was after the Treaty of Ghent ended the war, but before word of the treaty reached North America).

4. JAMES MONROE: First Seminole War (1817–18), against the Seminole Indians and fugitive slaves in Spanish Florida. General Andrew Jackson won a decisive, though brutal, victory, and convinced Spain that the United States could take Florida at will (which Spain gave the United States by treaty in 1819).

5. ANDREW JACKSON: Black Hawk War (1832), against the Sac and Fox Indians in Illinois and Wisconsin.

6. MARTIN VAN BUREN: Aroostook War (1839), against British Canada. U.S. and Canadian militias massed along the Aroostook River in the disputed territory between Maine and New Brunswick, but no blood was shed in this war. General Winfield Scott arranged a truce, and the crisis was settled by the Webster-Ashburton Treaty in 1842.

The Second Seminole War (ongoing). The Seminoles were fighting against their forced removal from Florida to the West. The last Seminole resistance ended in 1842.

7. JAMES POLK: Mexican War (1846–48), against Mexico. Following the annexation of Texas, relationships with Mexico became strained, and the border was undefined. When Mexico refused to sell California to the United States, war ensued. The Treaty of Guadalupe Hidalgo ended the war in February 1848. It set the boundary between the countries as the Rio Grande River; Mexico gave up territory that became all or part of the states of California, Nevada, Utah, Wyoming, Colorado, Texas, New Mexico, and Arizona; and the United States paid Mexico $15 million.

8. ABRAHAM LINCOLN: Civil War (1861–65). The war was precipitated by Lincoln's election, which caused the 11 southern states to attempt to secede from the Union. The capital of the Confederate States of America, Richmond, Virginia, fell in April 1865, and the Confederate General Robert E. Lee surrendered to Union General Ulysses Grant at Appomattox on April 9, 1865. Lincoln was assassinated by southern sympathizer John Wilkes Booth a week after the war ended.

9. WILLIAM McKINLEY: Spanish-American War (1898). Some say the war was caused by the efforts of journalist William Randolph Hearst looking for a story, others the explosion and sinking of the USS *Maine* in Havana harbor. Whatever the reason, it led to freeing Cuba from Spanish rule (Cuba was occupied by the U.S. military until 1902, and was a protectorate until 1934). The United States also took control of the Philippines, which were granted their freedom in the 1940s.

10. WOODROW WILSON: hostilities with Mexico (1913–17). Mexico went through a series of governments, none of which was able to consolidate control of the country. When the revolutionary

Pancho Villa raided across the border, killing people in New Mexico, Wilson sent General John J. Pershing in response, and he pursued Villa deep into Mexico. In February 1917, Wilson recalled Pershing to the United States, cooling some of the Mexican conflict, especially in light of the Zimmerman Telegram, which promised Mexico German support if the United States entered World War I against Germany.

World War I (1917–18). The war began in 1914, with an assassination in Austria-Hungary. Wilson's attempt to remain neutral was one of his campaign planks during his reelection in 1916. In 1917, Germany resumed unrestricted warfare against vessels in the Atlantic, sinking American ships. These acts, combined with the revelation of the Zimmerman Telegram, led Wilson to ask Congress, on April 2, for a declaration of war against Germany. On April 4, the Senate voted 82–6 to declare war. The House followed suit on April 6, 373–50. U.S. forces truly joined the war in 1918, and by November 11, 1918, when the Armistice was signed, U.S. casualties topped 300,000 killed and wounded. The Treaty of Versailles (1919) formally ended the war, placing full blame on Germany.

11. FRANKLIN ROOSEVELT: World War II (1941–45). The war began in 1939, when Germany invaded Poland. U.S. sentiment at the outbreak kept the country neutral. Increasing threats to Great Britain brought the United States closer to the Allied side, and a Japanese attack on the U.S. fleet at Pearl Harbor, Hawaii, on December 7, 1941, brought the country into the war. Roosevelt died in office on April 12, 1945.

12. HARRY TRUMAN: World War II (1945, see Roosevelt, above). Truman became President on April 12, 1945. Germany surrendered in May 1945, allowing the Allies to concentrate their resources on defeating Japan. Truman authorized the use of the atom bomb in order to prevent hundreds of thousands of Allied

casualties that would have resulted from an invasion of Japan. The first was dropped on Hiroshima on August 6, 1945, the second on Nagasaki three days later. On August 10, Japan sued for peace, and formally surrendered on September 2, 1945.

Korean War (1950–53). After Communist North Korean forces invaded South Korea in June 1950, Truman convinced the United Nations to unite to expel the Communists from the South. U.S. General Douglas MacArthur was placed in command of the multinational force, and Chinese troops came to the aid of the North Koreans. The war continued into Dwight Eisenhower's administration.

13. DWIGHT EISENHOWER: Korean War (1953, see Truman, above). Following his election in November 1952, Eisenhower visited Korea in December to revive stalled peace talks (which had begun in 1951). The Armistice was signed in July 1953, setting a demilitarized zone. As of 2008, no official peace treaty has been signed.

14. JOHN KENNEDY: Vietnam (1963). After unrest and the stirrings of war in southeast Asia, Kennedy sent military advisors to Vietnam, but refused to send combat troops. There is some evidence that he expected to withdraw all military intervention following the 1964 election. Kennedy was assassinated on November 22, 1963.

15. LYNDON JOHNSON: Vietnam War (1963–69, see Kennedy, above). Johnson escalated the U.S. role in Vietnam that began under Kennedy. There was no formal declaration of war, but the Gulf of Tonkin Resolution, which passed Congress almost unanimously, was taken as the legal basis for the United States to conduct the Vietnam War. The number of U.S. troops in the region peaked at 550,000 in 1968, and, though there were calls for peace talks, efforts in that direction seemed almost nonexistent.

16. RICHARD NIXON: Vietnam War (1969–74, see Kennedy and Johnson, above). Nixon reduced the number of troops, but expanded the region of war to include Cambodia and Laos. In 1970, the Senate repealed the Gulf of Tonkin Resolution (see Johnson), but a competing measure, to mandate withdrawal of U.S. forces, failed. National Security Advisor Henry Kissinger and North Vietnamese representative Le Duc Tho signed a peace agreement in Paris in January 1973.

17. GERALD FORD: Vietnam War (1974–75, see Kennedy, Johnson, and Nixon, above). Communist forces took over Laos, Cambodia, and Vietnam. Saigon, the capital of South Vietnam, fell in 1975, with the final evacuations of U.S. forces and personnel.

18. RONALD REAGAN: Invasion of Grenada (1983). U.S. forces invaded Grenada, ostensibly to protect U.S. lives, during a Marxist coup supported by Cuba. After removing the Marxists, U.S. forces left the island.

Hostilities with Iran (1987–88). Following escalating terrorist incidents worldwide, the United States and Iran engaged in several military skirmishes in the Persian Gulf.

19. GEORGE H.W. BUSH: Invasion of Panama (1989–90). U.S. forces invaded Panama on December 20, 1989, to capture General Manuel Antonio Noriega, who was in charge of the country, and who had been indicted in Florida on drug trafficking charges. Noriega was captured, and the operation concluded, on January 3, 1990.

The first Persian Gulf War (1990–91). On August 2, 1990, Iraq invaded Kuwait. Bush began Operation Desert Shield, to protect Saudi Arabia from further Iraqi aggression. Operation Desert Storm began with the bombing of Baghdad, Iraq, on January 17, 1991. On February 24, U.S. and Allied forces began a ground invasion of Iraq that lasted four days and removed Iraqi forces from Kuwait.

20. GEORGE W. BUSH: Afghanistan (2001–). Following major terrorist attacks on the United States in September 2001 (and see Reagan, above), for which the organization al Qaeda was deemed responsible, the United States attacked Afghanistan, ostensibly to find and punish those responsible. The attack also served to unseat the violently religious Taliban government, which had taken over that country.

The second Persian Gulf War (2003–). In 2003, the Bush administration convinced the world of the threat posed by Iraqi President Saddam Hussein's weapons of mass destruction programs (which later evidence showed were moribund or nonexistent), and invaded Iraq. Hussein was overthrown, arrested, convicted of mass atrocities against the Iraqi people in earlier years, and executed.

FIVE

AWARDS AND HONORS

E PLURIBUS UNUM

Naval Ships Named for U.S. Presidents

THE U.S. NAVY HAS A LONG HISTORY OF NAMING SHIPS AFTER Presidents. It goes all the way back to October 1775, when a 160-ton schooner originally named *Endeavor* was acquired by General George Washington for the Continental Navy and renamed for him. In 1799, a 28-gun frigate named for John Adams was launched. In recent decades, the navy has limited this practice only to the very largest, most expensive ships in the fleet.

The only non-nuclear vessel named for a President is the aircraft carrier USS *John F. Kennedy* (CV 67). The last non-nuclear carrier the navy built, the ship is currently listed as inactive. It was commissioned in 1968 and decommissioned in 2007.

The only non-aircraft carrier named for a President is the third and final *Seawolf* class submarine, the USS *Jimmy Carter* (SSN 23), named for the Naval Academy graduate and former submariner. It was commissioned in 2005.

The rest of the presidential ships are all *Nimitz* class aircraft carriers. They're nearly 1,100 feet long, 250 feet wide, and 240 feet tall from keel to mast. They weigh about 95,000 tons each, and carry crews of more than 6,000 (including 60 aircraft). At a cost of about $1.5 billion each, they may be the most expensive individual things named for specific people:

USS *Dwight D. Eisenhower* (CVN 69), commissioned in 1977.

USS *Theodore Roosevelt* (CVN 71), commissioned in 1986.

USS *Abraham Lincoln* (CVN 72), commissioned in 1989.

USS *George Washington* (CVN 73), commissioned in 1992.

USS *Harry Truman* (CVN 75), commissioned in 1998.

USS *Ronald Reagan* (CVN 76), commissioned in 2003, a year before her namesake's death.

USS *George H.W. Bush* (CVN 77). Her keel was laid in September 2003 and she was christened in October 2006, but at this writing hasn't yet been commissioned.

USS *Gerald R. Ford* (CVN 78) is scheduled to be the first aircraft carrier of a new class. Construction of the advanced ship is scheduled to begin in 2009. The ship was named prior to President Ford's death.

98

The Six Presidents on U.S. Coins

THIS LIST INCLUDES THE REGULAR-ISSUE, CIRCULATING COINS, EX-cluding special-issue medals and commemoratives (of which there were many). It does not include the new (as of 2007) presidential dollar coins, which are being issued four per year, depicting one new President each quarter of the year.

1. ABRAHAM LINCOLN. In 1909, to commemorate the centennial of Lincoln's birth, President THEODORE ROOSEVELT urged the U.S. Mint to replace the Indian Head cent with Lincoln's likeness (the Indian Head had been circulating for 50 years). Lincoln became the first U.S. citizen to be depicted on a U.S. Mint–issued coin. The original back was two sheaves of wheat surrounding the words ONE CENT. In 1959, the back design was changed to the Lincoln Memorial. The U.S. Mint plans major design changes for the cent in 2009—to celebrate Lincoln's bicentennial—though it will retain him on the coin.

2. GEORGE WASHINGTON. In 1932, to commemorate the bicentennial of Washington's birth, he became the second President depicted on a coin, when his likeness was placed on the quarter. He replaced a Standing Liberty design that had been in circulation since 1916. The back was a heraldic eagle, except for 1976, when the quarter, half dollar, and dollar coins received special Bicentennial backs (the quarter's was a drummer). The design remained unchanged until 1999, when the Mint instituted its "50 state quarters" program, issuing five different back designs each year (and redesigning the front to add more words).

3. THOMAS JEFFERSON. In 1938, Jefferson replaced the Indian Head front/Buffalo back (which debuted in 1913) on the five-cent coin. The new back of the coin was Monticello, the home Jefferson designed and built for himself in Virginia. The design was unchanged until 2004 when, seeing the success of the state quarters (and to celebrate the bicentennial of the Louisiana Purchase), the Mint issued two new back designs (one the peace medal Lewis and Clark gave to Indian tribes while representing Jefferson in their exploration of the Louisiana Purchase, the other a Lewis and Clark riverboat). In 2005, two further backs were issued (a buffalo, reminiscent of the coin Jefferson replaced,

and the Pacific Ocean), and the front was redesigned to a much more modern depiction of Jefferson. In 2006, Jefferson's image was changed yet again, to look out of the coin at the viewer (the back went back to Monticello).

4. FRANKLIN D. ROOSEVELT. In 1946, a year after Roosevelt's death, his image appeared on the dime, replacing the Winged Mercury head that had appeared since 1916. The back depicts a bundle of fasces (an imperial Roman symbol), which is a reimaging of the Mercury dime's back.

5. JOHN F. KENNEDY. In 1964, the year following Kennedy's assassination, public sentiment to put him on a coin overwhelmed the Mint's desire to not change coin designs within 25 years of their first issue. Benjamin Franklin, who first appeared on the half dollar in 1948, was replaced with Kennedy, and Franklin's Liberty Bell back was replaced with the Great Seal of the United States of America. In 1976, to celebrate the Bicentennial, the back was replaced with a depiction of Independence Hall.

6. DWIGHT D. EISENHOWER. In 1971, following Eisenhower's death and the first manned moon landing in 1969, the Mint brought back the dollar coin, which it hadn't minted since 1935. The same size as the earlier silver dollars, it wasn't made of silver, and proved too large for the average consumer to enjoy. Eisenhower was on the front, with the Apollo 11 mission logo on the back. For the Bicentennial, the back design was replaced, with the Liberty Bell floating in front of the moon. The coin design lasted only until 1978, when it was replaced with a smaller, but much vilified, dollar coin depicting Susan B. Anthony (the first actual American woman to appear on a U.S. coin) with a reduced version of the Apollo 11 logo on the back.

99

The Presidents on U.S. Paper Money

PAPER MONEY IN THE UNITED STATES WASN'T STANDARDIZED UNTIL after the Civil War. Before then, the only official national currency was coins. During that war, coins were hoarded for their metal content, and the federal government issued fractional currency: paper money with values of less than a dollar (George Washington appeared on several denominations of fractional currency, as did Thomas Jefferson). In 1869, the United States began printing paper money called United States Notes. These were followed by Silver and Gold Certificates, Federal Reserve Bank Notes, National Bank Notes, and, currently, Federal Reserve Notes. The Silver and Gold Certificates were promises by the government to redeem the notes for the equivalent in those metals; all the others were simply promises to pay, issued by the United States of America.

Paper money is issued by the U.S. Department of the Treasury, printed by the Bureau of Engraving and Printing, and has been issued in denominations of up to $100,000. The Federal Reserve System officially discontinued the use of bills greater than $100 in 1969 (the last of them were printed in 1945), and has withdrawn as many as possible from circulation. Only about 200 $5,000 and 300 $10,000 bills are known to exist.

1. GEORGE WASHINGTON (1789–97) is most often associated with $1 bills, though he has appeared on three different denominations. He started on the $1 United States Note issued between 1869 and 1923, then the Silver Certificates issued from 1896 to 1957, the Federal Reserve Bank Notes of 1918, and all Federal Reserve Notes since 1963. He also appeared on the $2 Silver Certificates of 1899, and the $20 Gold Certificates of 1905, 1906, and 1922.

2. THOMAS JEFFERSON (1801–09) appears on $2 bills, starting with the United States Note series of 1869 and continuing through 1963, as well as the Federal Reserve Bank Notes of 1918, and all Federal Reserve Notes since 1976.

3. JAMES MADISON (1809–17) has appeared only on $5,000 bills: the United States Note of 1878, Gold Certificates issued from 1870 to 1928, and Federal Reserve Notes starting in 1914.

4. JOHN QUINCY ADAMS (1825–29) appeared on the $500 United States Note of 1869.

5. ANDREW JACKSON (1829–37) has appeared on four different denominations. He started on the $5 United States Note series issued from 1869 to 1907. He was on $10,000 bills: United States Notes of 1878, and Gold Certificates of 1870, 1875, 1882, 1888, and 1900. Jackson was on several $10 bills: the United States Notes of 1923, Federal Reserve Notes of 1914, and the Federal Reserve Bank Notes of 1915, 1918, and 1929. He is currently best known for the $20 bill, on which he first appeared in the Gold Certificate series of 1928, followed by the Federal Reserve Bank Notes of 1929, the National Bank Notes of 1929, and the Federal Reserve Notes starting in 1928.

6. ABRAHAM LINCOLN (1861–65) has been on four different denominations, starting his career on $100 United States Notes in 1869,

1875, 1878, and 1880. He moved to the $500 Gold Certificates of 1882 and 1922. He was on the $1 Silver Certificate in 1899, and then finally found his home on the $5 bill: Silver Certificates from 1923 to 1953, United States Notes from 1928 to 1963, Federal Reserve Bank Notes from 1915 to 1929, National Bank Notes of 1929, and finally Federal Reserve Notes from 1914 to today.

7. ULYSSES GRANT (1869–77) has been on three denominations: He started on the $5 Silver Certificate in 1886, 1891, and 1896. At the same time, he was on the $1 Silver Certificate of 1889. His longest-lasting denomination, however, is the $50 bill. He started on the Gold Certificate series of 1913 and 1929, and then the Federal Reserve Bank Notes of 1929, the National Bank Notes of 1929, and the Federal Reserve Notes starting in 1914 and continuing to today.

8. JAMES GARFIELD (1881) served the shortest term of any President appearing on paper money. He appeared on the $5 National Bank Note of the Second Charter period, and the $20 Gold Certificate series of 1882.

9. GROVER CLEVELAND (1885–89, 1893–97) appeared on two denominations. He was on the $20 Federal Reserve Note series of 1914, the $1,000 Gold Certificates of 1928 and 1934, and the $1,000 Federal Reserve Note.

10. BENJAMIN HARRISON (1889–93) appeared on the $5 National Bank Notes of the Third Charter period.

11. WILLIAM MCKINLEY (1897–1901) appeared on the $10 National Bank Notes of the Third Charter period, the $500 Gold Certificate series of 1928, and all $500 Federal Reserve Notes.

12. WOODROW WILSON (1913–21) appeared on the $100,000 Gold Certificate series of 1934. This note never circulated, but was only used for transfers between Federal Reserve Banks.

100

National and State Capitals Named
for Presidents

TWO NATIONAL CAPITALS WERE NAMED FOR PRESIDENTS OF THE
United States.

1. Washington, District of Columbia, was of course named for
the first President, GEORGE WASHINGTON. The national capital
was originally New York City. It moved to Philadelphia in 1790,
and then to Washington in 1800. Second President JOHN ADAMS
was the first to serve in Washington.

2. Monrovia, Liberia. In 1821, the American Colonization Society founded Liberia as a haven for freed American slaves. The
first American Negroes arrived in 1822, and eventually, about
15,000 settled there. The colony became an independent nation
in 1847. Its capital was named for the man who was President
when it was founded, JAMES MONROE.

Four state capitals were named for Presidents (although one
of them hadn't yet been President when he was thus honored).

1. Jackson, Mississippi. Mississippi became a state in 1817, before
ANDREW JACKSON became President, but after he'd become fa-

mous by winning the Battle of New Orleans (in January 1815). Indiana was the first state to join the Union after the War of 1812 ended, in 1816; Mississippi was the second.

2. Jefferson City, Missouri, was named for THOMAS JEFFERSON. Missouri was the first state to be formed from the territory the United States acquired in the Louisiana Purchase, which was acquired during Jefferson's administration; it became a state in 1821.

3. Madison, Wisconsin, was named for JAMES MADISON. Wisconsin became a state in 1848.

4. Lincoln, Nebraska, was named for ABRAHAM LINCOLN. Nebraska became a state in 1867. Nebraska was the first state to join the Union after Lincoln was assassinated (indeed, before the states of the Confederacy were readmitted).

101

The Four Presidents on Mount Rushmore

MOUNT RUSHMORE NATIONAL MEMORIAL IS IN THE BLACK HILLS IN western South Dakota. It's a 5,700-foot-tall mountain carved to resemble the faces of Presidents George Washington, Thomas Jefferson, Theodore Roosevelt, and Abraham Lincoln (from left to right facing the mountain).

Historian Doane Robinson (1856–1946) came up with the idea of carving Mount Rushmore in 1923 to promote tourism in South Dakota. In 1924, he persuaded sculptor Gutzon Borglum to take the commission. Borglum had previously been involved in sculpting a massive bas-relief memorial to Confederate leaders (Stonewall Jackson, Robert E. Lee, and Jefferson Davis) on Stone Mountain in Georgia, but due to disagreements with the management, left the project.

(John) Gutzon de la Mothe Borglum was born in St. Charles, Idaho, on March 25, 1867. He trained in Paris, France, and then returned to the United States, where he sculpted many saints and apostles for the new Cathedral of Saint John the Divine in New York City in 1901. Borglum died of an embolism on March 6, 1941, seven months before work on his most famous sculpture was finished.

After Congress authorized the Mount Rushmore National Memorial Commission on March 3, 1925, President Coolidge insisted that, along with Washington, two Republicans and one Democrat should be portrayed. Borglum chose Jefferson, Lincoln, and Roosevelt, because of their roles in preserving the Republic and expanding its territory. The image of Jefferson was originally intended to appear in the area at Washington's right, but after the work there was begun, the rock was found unsuitable, so he was moved to Washington's left. The carving of Mount Rushmore started October 4, 1927, and ended October 31, 1941.

Washington's completed face was dedicated on July 5, 1934, Jefferson's in 1936, Lincoln's in 1937, and Roosevelt's in 1939. In 1937, a bill was introduced in Congress to add the head of civil rights leader Susan B. Anthony, but a rider was passed on an appropriations bill requiring that federal funds be used to finish only those heads that had already been started at that time.

Following Borglum's death in March 1941, his son, Lincoln, continued the project. The original plan was to sculpt the Presidents down to their waists, but it wasn't finished due to insufficient funding. Borglum had also planned a massive panel in the shape of the Louisiana Purchase, commemorating, in eight-foot-tall gilded letters, the Declaration of Independence, the Constitution, the Louisiana Purchase, and seven other territorial acquisitions from Alaska to Texas to the Panama Canal Zone. But the mountain itself required certain changes, such as moving Jefferson from Washington's right to his left, and Lincoln wound up in the place where the inscription was supposed to be (there was also the difficulty of carving the inscription large enough to be read). To replace the inscription, Borglum conceived of a "Hall of Records" to be carved into the back side of the mountain; a perfect place, he thought, to preserve important documents such as the Declaration of Independence and the Constitution. A chamber was cut 70 feet into the rock (far less than his original plans), but work stopped in 1941.

In 1998, the National Park System along with the Borglum family put the finishing touches on the Hall of Records. The room was not carved, but a titanium vault housing a teakwood box was installed in the granite floor in the entranceway. The box contains 16 porcelain enamel panels. On these panels are written the words of the Constitution, the Declaration of Independence, a history of how and why Mount Rushmore was carved, a history of the four Presidents with quotes from each, a biography on Gutzon Borglum, and the history of the United States. The capsule is sealed with a granite capstone bearing the words from one of Borglum's speeches.

The entire project cost $989,992.32.

On October 15, 1966, Mount Rushmore was listed on the National Register of Historic Places. In 1991, President George H.W. Bush officially dedicated Mount Rushmore.

SIX

OTHER PRESIDENTIAL
INFORMATION

The Most Uncommon Presidents (Those Appearing in the Fewest Lists in this Book)

CONSIDERING RANKED LISTS, FOUR ARE TIED WITH ONE APPEARANCE each. They appear in order of lowest ranking to highest:

1. FRANKLIN PIERCE (1853–57). He appears on only one list: The Presidents Who Outlived the Greatest Number of Their Successors. He is tied, with seven others, for the #3 rank, having outlived two of his successors.

2. DWIGHT EISENHOWER (1953–1961). He appears on only one list: The Five Presidents Who Issued the Most Vetoes. He is #4 on that list.

3. JIMMY CARTER (1977–81). He appears on only one list: The Five Presidents Who Lived Longest After Leaving Office. He is #3 on that list, though he'll move up to #2 on December 27, 2010.

4. ANDREW JACKSON (1829–37). He appears on only one list: The Presidents Who Had the Fewest Children. He is tied for #1 on that list, with four others, having adopted one child.

5. ANDREW JOHNSON (1865–69). He appears on only one list: The Five Presidents Who Had the Most Vetoes Overridden. He is #1 on that list.

6. GEORGE W. BUSH (2001–). He appears on only one list: Presidents Who Won Election by the Smallest Margins. He is #4 on that list, but his term is not yet finished at this writing, so he isn't yet included in several other lists on which he might rank.

Four others appear on two lists each: William McKinley (1897–1901) on lists 2 and 6; William Howard Taft (1909–13) on lists 5 and 16; Calvin Coolidge (1923–29) on lists 2 and 3: and Richard Nixon (1969–74) on lists 77 and 78.

103

The Most Common Presidents (Those Appearing in the Most Lists in this Book)

CONSIDERING ONLY RANKED LISTS, TWO ARE TIED WITH SEVEN appearances each:

1 (tie). GEORGE WASHINGTON (1789–97) appears on: The Five Presidents Who Died Soonest After Leaving Office (he's #3 on this list); The Five Tallest Presidents (tied for #5 with three others); The Presidents Who Had the Fewest Children (tied for #1 with four others); The Six Presidents Younger than Their Wives (#5); Presidents Who Won Election by the Largest Margins (#1);

The Presidents Who Issued the Fewest Vetoes (#10); and The Presidnets who Saw the Most States Join the Union (tied for #2).

1 (tie). RONALD REAGAN (1981–89) appears ons: The Five Presidents Who Lived Longest (#2); Presidents Older Than the Greatest Number of Their Predecessors (#1); Ten Presidents Who Were the Most Older Than Their Wives (#5 on the sublist of second wives); The Five Oldest Presidents (#1); Presidents Who Won Election by the Largest Margins (#5); The Five Presidents Who Were the Greatest Number of Years Older Than Their Predecessors (#1); and The Five Presidents Who Had the Most Vetoes Overridden (tied for #4 with one other).

3 (tie). Four Presidents appear on six lists each: Thomas Jefferson (1801–09) on lists 5, 28, 33, 77, 78, and 91; Zachary Taylor (1849–50) on lists 17, 28, 75, 79, 82, and 91; Millard Fillmore (1850–53) on lists 16, 30, 31, 32, 33, and 91; and Theodore Roosevelt (1901–09) on lists 2, 28, 32, 33, 76, and 80.

104

The Average President

AVERAGES TELL US ABOUT GROUPS AND ENABLE US TO MAKE PRE-dictions about any member of the group, but they can't tell us about the possibility for something new. Thus, any list of the average President will not help us predict the odds of a woman becoming President. Additionally, to come up with these averages, some Presidents have not been used (for instance, when calculating life span, the currently living Presidents were not included). With those caveats, we can calculate the average President. He (and looking at the 42 men who have held the office, the average President is 100 percent male):

★ Has a life expectancy of 70 years, 245 days (RUTHERFORD HAYES is the most average in this respect, having lived 70 years, 105 days)

★ Is five feet, ten inches tall

★ Has a better than one in four chance of being named James or John

★ Has a better than one in three chance of having been born in Virginia or Ohio

★ Has a better than one in three chance of being buried in Virginia or New York (after he dies)

★ Has an 18 percent chance of dying on the same day (but not year) as another President

★ Has a less than 10 percent chance of having no living predecessors

★ Has a 19 percent chance of being born in the same year as another President

★ Has a 16 percent chance of dying in the same year as another President

★ Has a 10 percent chance of being assassinated

★ Has a 7 percent chance of being born after his father's death

★ Has 3.7 children (2.1 sons and 1.6 daughters), of whom 2.3 will have children of their own, giving him 8 grandchildren

★ Is 5 years, 316 days older than his wife (THOMAS JEFFERSON is the most average in this respect; he was 5 years, 200 days older than his wife)

★ Has 1.15 wives

★ Will die 5 years, 183 days before his wife (WILLIAM McKINLEY is the most average in this respect; he died 5 years, 254 days before his wife)

★ Has a 40 percent chance of being Episcopalian or Presbyterian

★ Has a one in six chance that his father will be alive to see him inaugurated

★ Has a one in three chance that his mother will be alive to see him inaugurated

★ Has a 57 percent chance of being an orphan when he is inaugurated

★ Has a one in six chance of being known by a name other than the one he was born with

★ Has a 28 percent chance of being the firstborn child in his family

★ Has a 16 percent chance of being the last-born child in his family

★ Has a better than 50 percent chance that his father was some sort of farmer, planter, or landowner

★ Has a 38 percent chance that his father was a public official

★ Has a 50 percent chance of being a lawyer

★ Has a 50 percent chance of having served in a state legislature

★ Has a 45 percent chance of having been a state governor

★ Has a 42 percent chance of having been a member of the House of Representatives

★ Has a 36 percent chance of having been a senator

★ Has a one in three chance of having been Vice President

★ Has a 69 percent chance of having served in the military

★ Has a four in seven chance of being a Republican

★ Has a one in three chance of being a Democrat

★ Has a 29 percent chance of having attended Harvard or Yale

★ Has a one in six chance of not being a college graduate

★ Is 91.67 percent likely to win the vote of New Mexico in winning the election

★ Is 47.83 percent likely to lose the vote of Alabama in winning the election

★ Has a two in three chance of losing the vote of Washington, D.C., while winning the election

★ Is 55 years, 117 days old on inauguration day (WARREN HARDING is the most average in this respect; he was 55 years, 122 days old when he took the oath of office)

★ Has a one in four chance of serving two full terms

★ Will be President for 5 years, 60 days (LYNDON JOHNSON is the most average in this respect; he was President for 5 years 59 days)

★ Will veto 62 bills, and 2.5 of those vetoes will be overridden by Congress

About "President" David Atchison

David Rice Atchison represented Missouri in the United States Senate as a Democrat from October 14, 1843, to March 3, 1855. He is famous chiefly for the legend that, for one day in 1849, he was President of the United States.

Atchison was born on August 11, 1807, in Frogtown, Kentucky (now part of Lexington), went to school at Transylvania University in Lexington, and was admitted to the bar in Kentucky in 1829. In 1830 he moved to Liberty, Missouri, and set up practice there. In 1834, he was elected to the Missouri General Assembly, and reelected in 1838. In 1841 he was appointed a circuit court judge for the six-county area of the Platte Purchase, and in 1843 was named a county commissioner in Platte County, where he lived.

In October 1843, Atchison was appointed to the Senate to fill the vacancy left by the death of Lewis F. Linn. He was later elected to fill out Linn's term, and then reelected in 1849.

Atchison was very popular with his fellow Senate Democrats, and when they took control of the Senate in December 1845, they chose him as President pro tempore. He was only 38 years old, and had served in the Senate just two years. In 1849, Atchison relinquished the office in favor of William R. King. In December 1852, King, who had just been elected Vice President, yielded the office back to Atchison, and he held the post until December 1854.

The other senator from Missouri, Thomas Hart Benton, was also a Democrat, but he and Atchison found themselves on opposite sides of the slavery issue, and became political enemies. Atchison allied himself with the Whigs to defeat Benton in his bid for reelection in 1852. Benton came back to challenge Atchison's own reelection in 1854, and the Missouri legislature found itself split between the two, as well as a Whig candidate. Atchison's Senate term expired March 3, 1855, but Missouri failed to choose a successor until January 1857, when James S. Green was elected.

Following his Senate career, Atchison was a pro-slavery agitator, working (unsuccessfully) to get Kansas to join the Union as a slave state. In 1861, he accepted a commission as a general in the Missouri State Guard and led troops into battle for the Confederacy. Following a decisive Union victory in March 1862, he resigned from the army and retired to his farm near Plattsburg, Missouri.

INAUGURATION DAY, March 4, 1849, fell on a Sunday. Newly elected President Zachary Taylor refused to take the oath of office on a Sunday, so there was an interregnum, a gap between Presidents. Some claim that Atchison, as President pro tempore, was technically President of the United States for that day. Under the succession law in place at the time, following the President were the Vice President, President pro tempore of the Senate, and then the Speaker of the House of Representatives.

While amusing, there are several lines of reasoning which render this claim untrue.

First, if failing to take the oath of office meant that Taylor was not yet President, by the same reasoning, Atchison, who also did not take the oath, could not have been President.

Second, while President Polk and Vice President Dallas's terms of office had expired, so too had Atchison's as President pro tempore. He was still a senator, but the Senate was between terms, and at the time, Presidents pro tempore were elected as needed. Atchison was President pro tempore until March 4, and reelected again on March 5, but during the time there may have been an interregnum, there was no President pro tempore.

Atchison's "presidency," though fictitious, is not a new invention. In a September 1872 interview in the *Plattsburg Lever*, Atchison himself discussed it:

> It was in this way: Polk went out of office on the 3rd of March 1849, on Saturday at 12 noon. The next day, the 4th, occurring on Sunday, Gen. Taylor was not inaugurated. He was not inaugurated till Monday, the 5th, at 12 noon. It was then canvassed among Senators whether there was an interregnum (a time during which a country lacks a government). It was plain that there was either an interregnum or I was the President of the United States being chairman of the Senate, having succeeded Judge Mangum of North Carolina. The judge waked me up at 3 o'clock in the morning and said jocularly that as I was President of the United States he wanted me to appoint him as secretary of state. I made no pretense to the office, but if I was entitled in it I had one boast to make, that not a woman or a child shed a tear on account of my removing anyone from office during my incumbency of the place. A great many such questions are liable to arise under our form of government.

Atchison was 41 years, 205 days old at the time of his "presidency," making him the youngest President of all time. In order to beat his record, the President elected in 2008 will have to have been born after June 30, 1968.

Atchison died on January 26, 1886, and was buried at his home in Plattsburg, Missouri, where a statue honors him in front of the Clinton County Courthouse. His grave marker reads "President of the United States for One Day," although it does not have a presidential seal.

Index

Index of Presidents, Vice Presidents, and First Ladies appearing in this book, by chapter (Presidents appearing on ranked lists have the chapter number italicized).

PHOTO: © KIT HAWKINS

IAN RANDAL STROCK has been interested in the Presidents, history, and trivia for as long as he can remember. He earned a degree in political science from Boston University, then moved into a life of words: he works as an editor and writer. *The Presidential Book of Lists* is his first book, however his stories, articles, and trivia puzzles regularly appear in many magazines. Strock is the editor and publisher of *SFScope* (sfscope.com), which is the online trade journal of speculative fiction fields. He blogs about the Presidents, politics, trivia, and life in general at ianrandalstrock.livejournal.com.